Me, My Selfie, and I

Powder River Publishing

www.powderriverpublishing.com

Published by:
Powder River Publishing LLC
1014 Black Mountain Road
Thermopolis, Wyoming 82443

Copyright © 2022
ISBN: 978-1-956881-06-6
Printed in the United States of America

Dedication:

Dedicated to the memory of Thaddeus Aaron Davis, gone too soon.

Table of Contents

Chapter 1

Nahim pantomimed bouncing an imaginary basketball and performed various dribbling tricks using the balled up white socks he had retrieved from the floor as he flourished basketball techniques in the cramped bathroom space. He continued his announcing after and posting a layup into the laundry hamper. He missed. Lucky you're a good student. Otherwise, they'd revoke your black card, boy. After a beat, Nahim shook it off, picked up the socks, and started dribbling. Narrating, "Number twenty-two, Nahim Lightbourne. Nahim Lightbourne, ladies and gentlemen. A star four-sport athlete. He's captain of the basketball team. He also is a standout on the gridiron and on the diamond. Get this—he's even on the crew team. During his senior year, he's been named to the All-Conference team. Even more importantly Nahim is the textbook definition of a scholar athlete. He has a 4.0 grade point average and is in the running to be this year's valedictorian." "And the crowd goes wild!" Nahim stood there looking at himself in the mirror. He mimicked basketball moves—the between-the-legs bounce pass and Kareem Abdul Jabar's sky hook. H raised his arms in a victory pose and as he turned to flex, the light caught that little V from his chest down to his thing. I'm sexy! Who wouldn't want a piece of this? "You are a fine Black man."

He paused mid-flex and sadly asked himself "Why are you still a virgin? A seventeen-year-old star—who's never had sex? What's wrong with me? I'm the shit! I'm Nahim Lightbourne!" The bathroom door flung open. "What'd you say, boy?" He quickly reached for a towel to cover his naked body. "Mom!!! I'm naked!" He crouched a little worried that the towel was not going to do its job.

"Boy, you ain't got nothing I ain't never seen."

"But mom!" He whined and tried to duck behind the hamper.

"Pssh...you've seen one, you've seen them all. They all work the same way. Big, small, cut, uncut, soft or hard, they ain't nothing but trouble."

Lisa Ann Lightbourne, my mom, has always been open with me about everything. Truly outspoken, she often says what's on her mind. She does not mince words or sugarcoat. She did not really have a filter either. A few years ago, I had my appendix taken out. When I emerged from the anesthesia fog, she was shaking my willie and calling my name. The nurse had said I couldn't be released from the hospital until I peed. Groggy, I winced, "Mom, what are you doing?" Same response... "You've seen one, you've seen them all."

Her angry voice brought me back to the present moment.

"You ain't hear me calling you?"

"No ma'am. You've been calling me?"

"For the last ten minutes. If you'd turn that blessed music down maybe you could hear me calling your little nappy head. Just then, the lyrics of Childish Gambino's "Freaks and Geeks" rang out

"My dick is too big. There's a big bang theory."

Growing increasingly aware of my nakedness, I begged sheepishly, "Mom, can I get some privacy?"

"You want privacy? In my house? Ain't no such thing. I go where I want in my house. You've been spending too much time with them white folks you go to school with. Talkin' about 'Mom, can I get some privacy?' Her mimicry of white people always was accompanied by a stereotypical nasal sound. She laughed." Next you'll be asking for a time out instead of the ass whooping you gonna get if you ask me about some privacy again. Now get your butt downstairs and eat your breakfast before the bus comes and your little narrow behind gets left again. I ain't got time to drive you all the way out to that fancy school. I have to go to work."
I heard her mumbling from downstairs as she banged pots and pans. "Humph...privacy."

I had touched a nerve. I gotta tread lightly. Let me hurry up and get outta here. I ironed my clothes really quick. Just the front panels of the shirt. No one betta not say anything about my outfit. I hated wearin' this preppy stuff anyway. I'd rather just wear normal clothes, but khakis and button-down shirts were the school uniform.

I got dressed really fast and ran down the steps and threw my shoes on. I grabbed a bagel from the counter and spread some cream cheese on it. I practically swallowed the first half whole.

"Momma, you frying chicken already? It's not even eight o'clock in the morning." The air smelled like five o'clock in the evening.

"You wanna eat when you get home?"

"I just hate going to school smelling like grease. I am the only black kid there and I always stink up the bus smelling like dinner—like fried fish and greens."

"Ain't nothing wrong with fried fish and greens. That's just proof that your momma takes care of you. Your little friends probably smell like frozen pizza."

"Remember, I have that debate match against Harvest Prep. I won't even be home for dinner."

"You didn't tell me you had a match."

"Momma, the whole season's calendar is right here on the fridge." I walked over to the refrigerator to point at the schedule. It had been covered with the school artwork of my little brothers. The calendar was barely visible underneath all the Crayola rainbows and stick figures.

"Oh. Sorry, son. You need any money for food?" She reached for her purse setting on the counter. "I ain't got much." She started jingling through the loose change in her wallet.

"No ma'am. I'm good." I reached my hand towards her to stop her from counting." "Coach will buy dinner for the team on the way there."

"Oh, okay. Good luck tonight! Make me proud."

"Thanks, Ma." I stood up and packed up my backpack. I turned to leave out the side door.

"Uh, you forgetting something?"

I turned around and she was holding up my white J's.

Stupid. I grabbed the shoes from her hand and stuffed them into my bag. I reckoned it was not really about the shoes, so I leaned over and kissed her on her cheek. "Thanks, Ma. What would I do without you?"

"Where you goin' in them half-ironed clothes?" I acted like I didn't hear her and ran out the door.

"Bye, Ma. See you tonight." If I stayed much longer, she'd have me back at the ironing board for sure.

I arrived at the bus stop just as the bus was pulling up. I walked down the middle towards my usual spot near the back. It wasn't long before Westley reached over the seat as I shoved the other half of the bagel into my face. "Bean pie, my brotha?" He mimicked serving me a slice of pie. It was his fake black man accent that pushed my buttons. I should have jawed him right there! But then I'd be in the wrong. That accent frustrates me so.

What do you know about Black Muslims, you bastard? Westley thought he was so funny; the kids around him thought him hilarious. Their laughter shot through my nerves like that ALS ice bucket challenge. If we were on top of the school, I'da thrown him off the roof.

On away debate days, Coach required us to wear ties. When I put this bow tie around my neck, I should have thought it through that Westley's racist ass would say something. I am so tired of his little slights. I always have to be on guard around these folks. I never get to let my hair down. One of these days someone's going to catch these hands for saying some of that stupid cracker shit. I've become a case study in restraint. I work hard at not becoming what they don't want me to become.

I remembered my first day at this school. Mom felt I should "dress up" for the first day as my uniform had not arrived yet. I went into the cafeteria. The old lady checking IDs had the nerve to part her lips and say, "My! You dress nice for a colored boy." It didn't help that she had a Southern accent—just made the word "colored" sting all the more. Boy, I wanted to tell her off! But I had to think about where I was and who I was—the new guy—the new black guy. I calmed myself and responded "Ma'am. The term colored offends me. I identify as black. In future conversations, would you kindly refer to me as such?" That was three years ago, and, to this date, she has never called me colored again. I imagined how she'd gone home and called her family together and told them, "Listen, y'all. They ain't colored no more. They's black now."

I was getting used to being mistreated. That was my experience every place I entered-- every store I walked into. White clerks followed me and other black kids to catch us stealing. Meanwhile, the white kids were the ones robbing them blind! I used to want to be white—I mean, they get all the advantages. No stop and frisk. The benefit of the doubt. I thought like that until I saw for myself what they were really like. In the last ten years, almost all of the domestic massacres, school shootings, bombings, murders, you name it—yup, white people. I wish I could go out onto the roof of my building and scream "White people are messed up!"

And here I was thinking my mom was the one who was color struck. Of course, she did not have to attend this rich, lily-white school. Nor did everyone have to know she was the "affirmative action, diversity scholarship, "who only got in because he's smart" white guilt charity case. Every day, someone reminds me that I'm out of my habitus—out of my element. I get the "you don't belong here" stare wherever I go. Unfortunately, I also got that it in the 'hood from my own people. Once word got out that I attended Hilton Preparatory Academy, they started treating me differently. Chick told me that I thought my poop don't stink. I don't quite get that one, but a couple people around cosigned the comment. When the others on the stoop started calling me "Joe College" and "Braniac" I began to assume that being a smart, educated black man was an affront to both white and black folks alike.

I was at a crossroads and whichever path I chose would ruin someone's life. I'm pretty sure I would stick with the grin and bear it approach to which I had become accustomed. I should buy stock in Colgate Optic White toothpaste for all the grinning and shucking I feel I have to do daily. That toothpaste feels like your brushing with sand, but it works, and it is effective at removing stains and tartar buildup. But I'm telling you, Westley is cruising. I do not know how much longer I can keep frontin'.

Just as I was crafting ideas and fantasies about how Westley would meet his end; I heard the sweetest voice coming from a couple rows over. "I like your bow tie. It's very becoming."
I blushed (I think). Do black people blush? I must have 'cause all of a sudden my face got hot. Who is she? I've been riding this bus all year, but I have never noticed her.

"Hi. I'm Jolene Young. I'm new here."

I thought, Wow, that girl is thick as a Snickers!

Chapter 2

A year or so earlier, I found Momma tearing the house apart. She had to find the necklace before Daddy came home. Mom would prove to him that she knew he was cheating. She had found the pendant and chain mixed up in the blankets when she fluffed the covers to make the bed. She'd hid it, but once she retrieved it, she vowed to confront him and cuss him out; but the more she'd thought about it, she realized she needed more ammunition. He's a low-down, dirty snake but he would not cheat on me-- would he? Besides he was the king of the castle—the monarch--or so he liked to be called on the streets. I need real proof. I will have to catch him red-handed. I will never forget the day she came home from work early and found Daddy and his side piece in the throes. I think in Othello, Shakespeare described the scene as "an old black ram tupping your white ewe." Lord, did she have to be white?

As Momma walked through the front door, her antennae must have perked up. That's not how I left the pillows on the living room couch. She kept walking slowly towards the rear of the apartment. The way she'd described the events of that night, she'd heard sex noises emanating from the back bedroom. She quickened her pace to get to the door. I can only imagine how animated and amped she was to bust open the door. The moment she had been waiting for was finally here. "Ah hah! I knew it!" Dad bounced off the bed. As he fell, he waited for the hammer Momma held to be buried in his skull. But, Momma stopped mid- swing and turned and walked out the door and out of the apartment. Once Daddy came to himself, he found her note... "Pack your shit and go to that white bitch's house. Don't be here when I get back!" That's the story of how I became "man of the house."

That title, I would learn, came with responsibility, with pressure, with requirements for behavior, with constant reminders from mom every time I wanted to skip practice or not do my homework or play hooky. "Your brothers are looking up to you.

You're the man of the house now. You need to be better—to do better."

My older brother, Tyreek, had taken the wrong path in his life. Unfortunately, "the streets" got him several years ago. It all started when he befriended Blimpie. This dude, you could tell, was up to no good. He "smelled" shady. He had a bad reputation around the neighborhood as a guy who kept a pocketful of cash from ill-gotten means.

Tyreek began rolling with Blimpie and ignoring Momma's rules— staying out at all hours of the night, coming home when he felt like it. He started wearing the latest kicks— it seemed like a new pair each week. I know Momma didn't buy them. The stuff really hit the fan when the school resource officer came by the apartment and told Momma she was going to be fined if Tyreek kept being truant.

"Whatchu mean 'truant?' He leaves here every day going to school... at least that's what he says to me." Momma's left hand of defiance held tight to her hip, she read the paper with her right. She read aloud as if announcing the news 'The judge may (1) impose a fine on parents for truancy of up to three hundred dollars per offense, for the first offense, up to five hundred dollars per offense for the second offense and up to seven hundred and fifty dollars per offense, for a third and all subsequent offenses, (2) require parents to pay court costs, or (3) sentence parents to complete a parenting education program." Each time she mentioned a dollar figure her volume went up. Momma turned and looked at Tyreek; her eyes squinted as she peered at him. Her lips tooted out and she inhaled before she spoke again.

"Oh, thank you, Mister Policeman. We'll get to the bottom of this truancy matter." While attempting to appear polite, she practically pushed him out of the door.

Momma stood with her hand on the doorknob and her head staring straight down at the floor. She didn't say anything—she just stared—breathing. After a couple minutes passed, she peered out the keyhole—I think to make sure the officer had truly departed. When she felt satisfied, she let out an exasperated sigh...

"Boy! You got that white man coming to my house to tell me

I'm going to be fined because your ass ain't been going to school?"
All of a sudden, Momma lunged at Tyreek and began slapping him
all over his face and head. I heard various curse words and shouts
of Blimpie's name. The rest was pretty incomprehensible.

"Ma, chill!" Tyreek begged. Her physical tirade did not stop
though. She kept repeating the dollar amounts of the fines.
And that is when everything went off the rails. Tyreek grabbed her
hands and called her the name you never call a mad black woman—let alone your mom. "Bitch, I said stop!" And she did—mouth
agape with surprise.

"Oh no you didn't!" I could not tell if she was more stunned
by the word or the force of the accompanying shove. "I don't know
who you think you talking to. I ain't one of them suckas out on
the streets. Blimpie gonna get you killed." At that she leaped at
him with the force of a crouching tiger. The fury of her punches
seemed more appropriate for the octagon rather than living room.
Tyreek did little more than put up a defensive posture. How mom
got slapped is unknown.

"Oh, it's like that?" She put her hands down in defeat. "Oh,
you grown now? I can't whoop a grown man; I'll have to fight you
ass like a grown man. You need to leave." At that, she walked
nonchalantly over to the door and swung it wide to the left. She
stood to the side of the door with her right hand in church usher
position. Tyreek took the hint. As he departed, I overhead him
speaking on the phone.

"Yo, Blimp! Come pick me up. This chick over here trippin'.
What you mean 'Who?' My momma just put me out. Bring the
truck."

Tyreek started to walk in the direction toward our bedroom.
"Where you going?"
"I'm going to pack my stuff."
"You ain't got no stuff. Everything you own is because of
me. I paid for it. I own it."
Mimicking momma, "Oh, it's like that?" His incredulous
look bespoke betrayal and disappointment.
"Yup, it's just like that. You hit me. You think you're a man
now, huh? That you're grown? We will see how grown you are out
in them streets you like so much. You think Blimp is gonna let you

stay with him indefinitely? I bet he will kick you to the curb as soon as you leave a pair of your dirty drawers laying on the floor like you do here. Or, until he finds a new sucka to sell his rocks for him... Yeah, I know that's what you have been doing. You think you are nickel slick. I ain't stupid. Your daddy thought I was stupid, and you see where he is? Not here. And you can go join him. Don't let the doorknob hit you where the Good Lord split you." Momma's right arm and index finger showed the way for Tyreek to go. He tucked his tail but still stubbornly tried to pimp his way out the door like it didn't matter. I know his feelings were hurt. His pride too, I imagine.

"Bye, 'Reek." I whispered somewhat as I watched my first hero take the walk of shame. He feigned trying to be "da man" but I know he just wanted to grab his mommy by the ankles and beg to stay. Man code, however, would not let him admit fault nor defeat.

I was ten when she put daddy out and thirteen when she showed Tyreek the door. Momma was clearing her life of the men of the house. I wondered if I was next given my new title. I pledged internally to not disappoint her. She deserved someone to remain true to the promise and to the vision.

I didn't want the prescription to be true for Julian and Malcolm that had befallen me. I wanted to give them someone to look up to-- a dream to aspire to. The streets took my daddy and my big brother, but they were not going to get me.

I had been blessed by the gift of basketball; I played most of my life. AAU, the traveling squad—all of it. I had amassed a little following in middle school. That's when I met the recruiter from HPA. I started ninth grade at Hilton Prep . I knew it would be a sacrifice for momma to foot the tuition even with a scholarship.

"Don't you worry about what it costs, baby. You are worth it. I will figure it out."

So, that's why I have not knocked Westley's teeth out. It's why I put up with these white people's bull. It's why I do not go off when these stupid chicken head girls want to touch my hair decrying how it feels like steel wool. Like they even know what steel wool feels like. They probably have never scrubbed a pot in their spoiled little lives.

Chapter 3

Not going to lie. I'm sure I stick out like a sore thumb at Hilton Preparatory Academy. It is not like PS #62, the Langston Hughes High School. At Langston it was wall to wall niggas. Everybody there looked just like me. They wore baggy, sagging jeans and too large t-shirts—just like me. Yup, sneakers too. The girls kept their hair "did." Up dos, finger waves, weave and wigs of all colors and styles. Like it or not, these were my people. I was one of many and could easily blend into the crowd.

That is not my experience at Hilton. I am a speck of pepper in a mountain of salt—a baby scoop of chocolate in the giant vanilla sundae. These fancy white kids get away with whatever they want. Westley and his crew were always skipping classes and they tried repeatedly to get me to join them. I tell them I do not do things like that. Sure, I have earned the reputation for being a goody goody, but they probably would never understand the fact that teachers—no matter how large or small the class size—could tell that the speck was not in class. To say I am conspicuous is an understatement.

These kids were just like the ones in the movies. I've noticed the patterns juxtaposing white kids in school versus the black and Latino educational experience. Black and brown kids are violent, drug-addicted, gang-affiliated, drug dealers who can't read and their schools are under threat of state government takeover if the students don't pass the minimum standards test. White schools are palaces on sprawling campuses with trees and grass. The sun is always shining. White kids drive BMWs and Mercedes. Their only worry is how to lose their virginity on prom night or before graduation. If the movie is set in a high school, the students are awaiting their Ivy League college acceptance letters. If it is set on a college campus, the students are preparing to graduate and go to work in their fathers' Fortune 500 company on Wall Street or they are applying to law school or medical school. There's no such thing as supervision—parental or otherwise. At Langston, the cops were in the classrooms often in battle gear.

I am never more noticeable than during Black History Month when the teachers decide to finally mention a black person who was not enslaved or a victim of oppression. Or when they talk about race at all. It's funny. When the subject of race comes up, all heads swing in my direction—even if we are not talking about black people. Hell, we had a special topics class on the subject of whiteness and how whiteness is lived in America and no one talked except me and the Chinese international student who was "fresh off the boat" (as Westley was fond of saying).

Black American history (a misnomer of sorts as teachers rarely imagine blacks as Americans. Vestiges (yes, I know fifty cent words) of "separate but unequal" for sure. Black history as taught at Hilton can be summed in a five seconds—blacks came in chains as slaves, Abraham Lincoln set them free, Rosa Parks sat down, Martin Luther King dreamed... Obama won the presidency. Precious little else was taught or imagined.

During my sophomore year, Mrs. Greenawald, the history teacher, dared to show the entirety of the televised version of Alex Haley's Roots (nearly ten whole hours). I got into a skirmish just about every single day we watched that movie because some smartass would call me Toby and challenge me asking 'What's your name, boy?' Momma understood though. She did not even get mad at me for fighting in school. She said the same thing happened to her in the seventies when the movie first came out on television. The kids called her "Kizzy."

"Just be careful, son. Don't let them white people get you all riled up." Momma reassured me they would forget about the film soon enough. She was right—at least temporarily.
It is the literature that gets these fools all twisted. It is hilarious to me to watch them get tongue tied trying to avoid reading the

word "Nigger" in Huckleberry Finn. Kyle was like "I cannot say that word." *I'm thinking Quit frontin'. You know you use that word all the time. I know you listen to hip hop.* Some of the parents tried to get the book added to the Banned Books list 'because its use of the "N-word" was not "inclusive" and made students uncomfortable. I bet the only reason it is "uncomfortable" is because my black ass is setting right there among them.

Mrs. Berger-McBurney first introduced me to *To Kill a Mockingbird* by Harper Lee during freshman year. Great book but being the only black kid in the class while we read it was hard. Admittedly, we read it shortly after Trayvon Martin was killed by George Zimmerman. Imagine going to the store for some Skittles and ending up dead. So, yes, I was a little sensitive.

She had introduced it as "the perfect book—the perfect vehicle" for discussing everything she thought was important: integrity, equality, and empathy. At some point it got to be a little much and I asked Berger-McBurney if I could leave the room as she discussed the historical context of the word "nigger." Trembling, she looked at me and asked if I was okay. I told her "I'm okay, just a little uncomfortable." When she gave me leave, I almost went into full-on sprint into the hallway.

What is going on with you Nahim? Get it together. Remember how your momma said to not let them get to you? In frustration, I banged my head against a nearby locker. When I went back into the room, Berger-McBurney asked the class "What do you think Lee meant when she wrote 'You never really understand a person until you consider things from his point of view... Until you climb inside of his skin and walk around in it.'?" I stopped. Was she talking to them about me? I buzzed from head to toe. This book might be too much too soon for these young impressionable stupid minds.

I wanted to like Atticus. He seemed like an alright white dude, but could Tom Robinson escape the accusation of raping that white girl? Atticus plainly revealed that she was telling a boldfaced lie— her and her drunk, hillbilly redneck daddy. Yet, despite his innocence, Tom was convicted. Forget that "innocent until proven guilty" nonsense. Tom was a black man in AmeriKK-

Ka. He did not even stand a chance. His death was expected. Similarly, Zimmerman served as judge, jury, and executioner of young Martin. Trayvon was profiled and presumed guilty by Mr. Zimmerman, a self-appointed neighborhood watchman. Some idiot in my class, Kennedy Noble, had the audacity—the unmitigated gall—to part his lips to add "Zimmerman is not being treated fairly. It's not right. They are bullying him—the media, the NAACP, even the President of the United States is trolling him." By the time Jamison Bond chimed in with "A white man can't catch a break!" I was through!

"Are you serious?" I pounded the desk and stood over him— intentionally trying to appear more menacing and intimidating. "Who is dead here?" I blared. I dammed the salt flow from escaping my eyes. *You better not cry, punk!* "Trayvon's only guilt was wearing a uniform we all recognize— black skin and a dark hoodie. Zimmerman is a racist!"

"He was just protecting his neighborhood" Matthias shot out.

"Protecting them from who? From what? There was nothing for him to be suspicious of. A black boy out late at night in a nice neighborhood—so, he deserved to die for that? Zimmerman was the aggressor. He followed Trayvon. Or, should I say, he hunted Trayvon? Then he claimed the shooting was self-defense. Ain't that a bunch of horse shit? Ooh, sorry Mrs. B."

"But George Zimmerman had every right to ask Trayvon what he was doing in that neighborhood. He was just doing his job." Becky's justification just pissed me off.

"And therein lies the problem. That was not his job. George Zimmerman is not the law. He is not even a police officer. But he was armed — with a handgun, a prejudice and very bad judgment. He racially profiled, he followed, he engaged—even after the real police told him to stand down." I am running out of patience with these people.

Over the next few weeks, students were up in arms about Trayvon's murder. There were kids getting in trouble for wearing hoodies which broke the dress code. In my digital photography class, I took a picture of myself with a hoodie on and swirled my face using Photoshop. I uploaded it to Facebook using the caption "What Zimmerman Saw." Some students reacted negatively. Some of those had the nerve to be part of the protests. Bunch of hypocrites!

Mrs. B. tried to steer the conversation back to *To Kill a Mockingbird*. "Maybe we should talk about the book?"
"I retorted. "We are talking about the book. Tom did not get a fair trial because he was a black man. And neither did Trayvon Martin for the same reason. And this dude is probably gonna get away with murder because he's white."

Jamison jumped back into the conversation, "But Zimmerman's not even white. He is Latino."

"What?" I let slip loudly. "What are you talking about? Yo, you sound stupid. Stop talking."

"No, really. I heard on the news that Zimmerman is mixed race. He is Hispanic and white."

"Hispanic and what?"

"White."

"Exactly." Sarcasm would not be lost today. "George Zimmerman. He is as Hispanic as Goldfarb over there."

Now I am forced to contend with side glances and the more than occasional slight—except when I am balling out on the court. I am a beast in the paint. I go hard all four quarters. I run circles around those prep schoolboys. Honestly, they are not worth holding my jock strap. Coach even tells them "Get the ball to Lightbourne."

Chapter 4

It had become clear to me that these white people did not see me. They did not even think of me as a real person. I was their basketball star brought on to prove they weren't be racist. Look, there he is right there. And he is a scholarship kid. We are not racist. We are good people. I could tell they only had one expectation for me and for my future. They were not thinking about my someday going off to college; they were expecting me to just go back to wherever I came from—back to the rock I had crawled out from under.

As expected, in July 2015, George Zimmerman had been found not guilty. I dreaded the thought of going back to Hilton Academy where the white folks now had their proof of Trayvon's guilt. The media had crucified him. Someone had gone back through his Twitter account and had drudged up his tweets about rap music and sex. The image of him as a smooth faced seventeen-year-old kid had been transformed into a tattooed menace who had a drug problem because he had an empty marijuana bag in his school book bag. It is no wonder Zimmerman was "scared" because Martin fit the description.

When the new school year started, I determined I was not going to let these white folks win. I would prove to be an exception to the rule. Following my printed schedule, I walked into room B-twenty on the lower floor and down the long hallway. The schedule dictated I would be in American Studies with Davis. When I entered the classroom, I saw him. Well, I noticed his faded haircut from the back of his head as Davis wrote on the blackboard. I stood in the doorway—stunned--Hilton Prep Academy had hired a black teacher. The classroom filled with equally surprised students. The second bell rang as I found my way to a seat in the middle of the classroom.

Davis dropped his chalk into the tray and clapped the dust away. "Good morning, class." His baritone voice pushed away the silence in the room. "I am Dr. Thaddeus Aaron Davis." He paused before speaking again. "I am a little old school. If someone says, 'Good morning.' You answer back. Now, good morning class."

A choir of "good mornings" rang out in unison. Davis continued his introductions, "I earned my doctorate in African American Studies from Temple University under the leadership and tutelage of Dr. Molefi Asante, one of the nation's most distinguished contemporary scholars in Afrocentric thought and as one of the ten most widely cited African Americans. Now, that may not mean anything to all of you, but I am incredibly honored to have worked under the mentorship of such a scholar." He paused and wiped at the corner of his left eye. "You see," his voice cracked a little, "where I come from, very few people go to college. I am the first person in my family to earn a Ph.D., for that matter, even go to college, so for me to have earned this title is pretty significant." By then, his eyes had filled with tears and he could hardly control how shaky his voice got.

He took a couple seconds to compose himself. When he could continue, he held up a clipboard and took roll. "Let's see who we have here. If I ruin your name, please forgive me. Correct me and help me say it correctly. Anchorstar, Didrik? Borja, Alexis?"

"You can call me Lexie." Lexie brushed the brown locks from her face while she talked.

Dr. Davis called a bunch of other names before announcing my name. Lightbourne, Nahim?"

"That's me, sir." I raised my right hand.

"Lightbourne? I grew up with a guy named Lightbourne. We used to call him 'The Monarch.' You know him?"

"Actually, I do. He's my father." I was so surprised that we had a connection—me, the only black kid at this school and Doctor Davis, the only black teacher at Hilton Prep Academy—connected through my dad.

I heard a couple of whispered snickers, "Monarch? Like the butterfly?" I glared in the direction of the whispers.

"I haven't seen ole Monarch in years. How's he doing?" Davis smiled as he inquired. It was obvious he had fond memories.

"Honestly, that's the same for me." I hated to be this open about my family's secrets in front of these rich snobs. I felt ashamed all of a sudden.

"Well, let's talk after class today. Your dad and I go way back. Boy, I can tell you some stories!" He continued the roll call.

"Marth, Nicholas. McCloskey, Christian. Person, Westley."

"Yo, wassup Doc?" Westley answered in his usual rendition of black vernacular.

"Let me stop you right there, sir. I'm not your friend, your bro, your homie, your fam, or anything else that you the music videos have taught you about black people and the way they speak. The name is Dr. Davis, and I fully expect you to address me in that way. Looking down over his glasses, "Understand me, sir?"

"Yes sir. Sorry, sir." *Oh, I like this guy already.* My first black teacher at Hilton and he put Westley in his place!

Charles Wynn was the last name on the roster. When Dr. Davis finished taking names, he adjusted his tweed jacket with the suede patches on the elbows and walked to the front of his desk. He grabbed a stack of papers from the corner and began passing down the rows giving each person his or her own.

With the authority of a statesman, Davis began to address the class. His stern tone suggested that he was a man not to be messed with. "This is American Studies. Our main objective in this course is to better understand the varied peoples who inhabited what came to be the United States from the era of overseas expansion through the end of the Civil War and Reconstruction. We will come to know them through a study of the critical events and the social, political, and intellectual currents which shaped their lives and created the foundations of our own society today." Davis continued, "This course will help you to understand the forces shaping human behavior, social structures, and institutions as they developed in our nation. We will examine the ethical values of the individuals we study, trying to understand why individuals and groups of people made the decisions they did within the context of their times. We will notice how many events from the past bear directly on the advantages and challenges of our own generation. We will see how historians borrow from other disciplines such as ecology, anthropology, and literature to draw a better picture of the past."

He stopped reading and asked the class "Who is an American?" Students began timidly raising their hands as they turned and looked confusedly at each other. Assuming their confusion, he rephrased the question. "I mean, what is an American? Maggie?" Surprised to be being called on, Maggie sat up in her chair. "Someone who was born in America?"

"Okay, that is true, but not necessarily what I meant." His smile warmed the room. "What does it mean to be an American? What is American culture?"

He entertained a few more comments from the students. Several spoke of freedom and liberty—about America being the "land of the free and the home of the brave."

Davis chimed in, "Being American means to be a part of a whole. On the back of our money is the Latin phrase e pluribus unum. Who knows what that means?" He answered before anyone spoke 'From many, one.' According to what we have been taught, we are free to believe how we choose— this constitutionally protected 'freedom of religion.' So, no matter what deity you worship (or not) you are welcome here supposedly. Being American is not necessarily about living in America. America has got to mean something more than just the borders, something deeper and more important.

He turned the page and continued reading:
"In a practical vein, in this course you will develop skills necessary to succeed in your college courses. In fact, this course is going to feel like a college level history course, at times. We'll study history, anthropology, sociology, and the arts as we try to ascertain this notion of American-ness. You will have opportunities in this course to research, to make judgments about sources, to write in a scholarly style, and to think critically and to make a formal presentation."

"In recent years, there has been a clarion call for us to 'go back' to better times as a country. Whenever there is a hot- button topic of discussion like gun control or voting rights, pundits refer-

ence the language of the Constitution of the United States as sac-
rosanct." Pointing matter-of-factly at me, he affirmed, "Nahim,
the Constitution was not written for us. Maggie, Lexie, Madison,
it was not written for you either. He surveyed the classroom with
his eyes, "I am here to remind you all how this important docu-
ment was written at a time when people those of us who weren't
male and white were not even considered American. In fact, people who looked like me weren't even considered a whole human.
Who knows what percentage of a human being black people were
considered?" No one answered.

"Three fifths. President James Madison, one of the fram-
ers of the Constitution was the one who codified African slaves as
three fifths of a human. Imagine—three fifths of a human being.
Which parts are those? Ponder that for a second. And Madison
himself along with eleven other presidents were slave owners."
Incredulous, the chatter was one of surprise at this new information. Davis gave time for the commotion to settle. After a few
moments of silence, Davis continued reading from the syllabus.
"During the second half of the semester we will read portions of
published slave narratives of your choice. Two assignments will
be based on your readings. First, you will write a four-to-five-
page essay on a related topic based on your research into these
slave narratives. More details on the requirements for the paper
will be provided. Second, in groups of three to five students who
chose the same topic, you will synthesize the research you did for
your paper and create a formal, ten-minute group presentation in
which you will share your conclusions with the class. Expectations
for the presentation will also be provided later in the semester.
Each student will receive an individual grade for the group presentation."

Didrik grumped, "I hate group assignments." Several others joined the chorus of dislike for group work.

"I know, I know." Davis waved both his hands. "I hate
group work as well. There is always someone who doesn't pull
their own weight yet still benefits from everyone else's work."
So many people agreed it felt like a Pentecostal service at a black
church. I swear I heard someone say "Amen."

"Well, I think I have figured out a solution. Group members will have the opportunity to fire any group member not sharing in the workload. To fire someone, you will have to write a letter of complaint to me addressing what the person is or isn't doing and make a recommendation that person be fired. Let me make this clear, anyone who is fired will fail the assignment and not have the opportunity to work alone as this is a collaborative learning assignment. Does everyone understand?"

Voices rang out, "Yes, Dr. Davis."

"Good. This paper I am passing out right now has all of the requirements outlined as I have explained them. Take this home and let your parents read it. You and they should sign it and return it to me."

The bell rang to indicate class change. I felt instantly depressed. I did not want to leave. I just knew this man was going to change my life here at Hilton. I stood up to make my exit.

"Mr. Lightbourne." I stopped in my tracks and looked to the front of the room. "Hang out for a few minutes."

Chapter 5

"I like your bow tie. It's very becoming."

What a sweet voice. A chill ran down my spine; I shivered.

"Thank you." I adjusted the tie a little—concerned it had become crooked while I ran towards the bus. All of a sudden, I heard momma's challenge about wearing "rough dried clothes" anytime I ironed the way I did this morning." In my self-consciousness I smoothed the wrinkles.

I'll be honest. Compliments at Hilton Academy don't come my way very often—off the court, that is. On the court, fans seem to come out of the woodwork--especially rich white men. They say things like, "We're so glad you came to our school." "You're such a natural. One guy said, ""Black people are so cool. I wish I was black." After one game, an older white lady said to me, "I just love you people." She was probably related to Westley.

But, here was a pretty white girl my age looking at me and telling me I was handsome. I think I watched her the entire rest of the bus ride to school. I had to play it off like I was not looking, so I kept my head turned towards the windows and stole glances when the bus hit a bump or shook. Thank goodness for book bags. Mine made for good cover as I let my thoughts wonder about the mysterious new girl on my bus.

When we got to school and out of earshot, I leaned over towards Tucker and put my arm around his shoulder. Tuck was one of the cool white boys. He was down. I felt safe with him. I questioned, "Dude, did you see that new girl get off the bus? She was fine!"

"I saw her, Bro! Damn... she shapoppin'." Clearly, he had been studying the Urban Dictionary again. "I wonder what her situation is."

"How can we find out more info about her?" I was surprised by my own inquisitiveness. Desperate times.

"What's the point? Even if you did get her number, you'd

chicken out and not call her."

"Nope. Not this time. I need to make her wifey."

"Whatever dude. " His sarcasm was biting.

"I admit it. I have chickened out in the past, but I think I'm ready now. I'm pent up. I need to release the pressure—if you get what I am putting down."

"Clear as day, friend. Clear as day. I can totally appreciate what you're saying. Before Camille, I was in the same boat. Tired of adjusting the antenna, huh?"

"I am my own best friend," I snickered.

"Don't worry, we'll get you booed up. I'll ask Camille to hook you up. But, you better not do the Nahim again."

"Dude, I'm serious. Let me work that Lightbourne magic on her. Give me a month. She'll be sprung. One month. That is all I need."

"You'll mess it up."

"You want to bet?" I challenged.

"What do you want to bet? What do you have to bet?"

"That's cold."

"I didn't mean it that way. I'm sorry, bro, but seriously, what's the bet?"

"In one month's, time, I'll have her swingin' off my jim- my."

"And when you don't, what do I win?" His doubt was get- ting tiring. I huffed.

"If I am not tappin' that this time next month, I will be your in-school slave."

"Ooh, you must be serious. You don't even like that word in school. You get mad when the history teachers use it."

"You think it is a joke, don't you, Tuck? That girl will be mine, just you wait. I will be hittin' that in no time!"

"Yeah, I know you think you will." Tucker held us his right hand to give me a high five. I slapped it and pulled him in for some real dap.

"Will you all just get a room for goodness sakes? You are the huggin-est boys I have ever seen. If Tuck was not mine, I would be wondering if you all were on the LGBTQ spectrum."

"Naw, naw, naw...You can keep that mess. I ain't about the butt and balls life. I am a kitty lover--meow. Keep pressing your luck and I might have to clean you with my tongue."

"Hey, hey now! That's my lady you are talking to. Put some respect on it!"

"Sorry, bro. No disrespect intended. Just making sure your girl knows the real."

"I get it. Nahim is a man's man. I should not have said what I said." She paused for a second. "What are you all hugging out this time?" She faced us both with an inquisitive look on her face.

"Nahim's got a crush."

"Crush? Dude I am positively in love. Did you see her in that little Catholic school girl skirt? She looked like she jumped out of the Britney Spears' video."

"For real? Who?" She pushed me as if she heard something impossible.

"This new girl on the bus this morning. See if you think can get her phone number and pass on to our boy here? He is getting desperate."

I could have done without the head rub.

Later that day after twelfth period, Camille approached me and handed me a small slip of paper. "What is this?"

"Her name is Jolene Young and that's her phone number. She just transferred here from Trinity School. I mentioned that you were interested."

"You did WHAT?" I interrupted. "I did not tell you to tell her that. All I wanted you to do was get her digits. Now you got this girl thinking I'm interested.... What she say?" I coyed.

"She said you're cute."

"How did she know who I was?"

"Really, dude? You do kinda stick out around here. You are a little obvious—even without me mentioning you."

I laughed because it was true.

"She wants you to call her tonight between seven and eight thirty. She said those specific times and not a minute sooner or later."

"Why so specific?" I wondered.

She said her dad is super religious—a pastor at that—he has some kind of church function tonight and she will have the house to herself for that time."

"What? A preacher's kid! Well, hallelujah hot dog! You know what they say about PKs? She's probably got a tramp stamp. I will be hittin' those skins next week!"

"Nahim!" Camille scolded.

"You know pastors' daughters are freaks." Pausing to consider, "She's a for real for real pastor's daughter?" I smirked. Immediately, my thoughts went toward a girl who has low morals and strict parents. "I hope she's a loose girl who likes to rebel because of her father's job and strictness. I'll be her rebel toy."

"Nahim, that is an awful stereotype. You of all people should know how stereotypes hurt."

"Why me of all people?" I am just wondering if she's the good kind or the bad kind. I hope it is the latter. I am hoping she is the bad kind of those girls who go against everything that their daddy preaches. Those girls who sneak out of the house and get drunk on the weekends and are somehow perfect and pristine when they walk into the church on Sunday morning. Hmmm... I wonder if she is the kind who likes to speak with tongues." I flicked my tongue several times and then I straight cackled at that.

"You, sir, are a pig! I only talked to her for a few seconds, but she seems legit. I think she is the real deal 'The good kind' as you call it. And if she is, I would hope you would respect that and not try to ruin her."

"I am not going to ruin her. Not gonna lie, though, I hope her daddy preaches submission."

"I didn't' know you were so nasty. I thought you were one of the good men, but, you are just a man." The disappointment showed on her face.

"I get what you're saying," I mumbled. "I will text her first to make sure everything is all clear. I will let you know how it goes. See you later."

Basketball practice seemed to take forever. It was six thirty by the time I got done with the fifty suicides Coach made us run

because so many of the guys on the team were failing their classes. The bus comes at six forty-five. I didn't have enough time to
take a shower before running to the stop. It will take at least an
hour for me to get home. I hope I won't miss my window. Better
yet, I hope Jolene invites me to her window.

Magically, the bus got me home in exactly fifty-five minutes. I ran in and took a quick shower. I did not want Jolene to
smell me over the phone. I texted "Hi. It's Nahim. Sorry... long
practice. Still got time to talk?" When I pressed send I hoped to
hear that beep immediately. I kept the phone in my hand and
stared at it—willing it to beep.

I set the phone down and went to pee right quick-- nervous
bladder. As soon as the flow started flowing, I heard the ding.
"Shoot! Hold on, baby. I will be right there."

It is almost impossible for a man to cut off the stream—
without pain, that is. I barely had time to tap tap at the end as I
was so excited to get back to the phone.

"Dad home soon. No time to talk. Will see u tmrw. Sit with
me on the bus."

"Dang it." I returned. "Okay. Hasta manana. Gnite."

Chapter 6

When I woke up, Momma was in the kitchen listening to the television news. The scroller read "It's Election Day. Get out and vote!" Momma was already dressed. No robe and rollers. Momma took voting seriously. Every year, she packed up all the kids and traipsed us down to the polling place. She actually took us in the booth with her. All of us kids. The poll workers knew us by name and announced us as we walked in the room. "The Lightbournes are here!" Momma's face always swelled with pride and she Cheshire Cat-smiled every time.

She gave us the same speech every single time—primaries and general elections. "Kids, this is probably the most important thing we do as Americans—as black Americans especially. There was a time, when black folks were not allowed to vote. Our forefathers fought, bled, some even died trying to vote. All of those enslaved ancestors who worked in the cotton fields who were denied basic human rights-- We vote because they couldn't."

"Momma, it's Election Day" I announced as I walked in the room.

"I know it's Election Day, boy. Why do you think I am up and dressed and ready so early this morning? The boys are dressed and ready. They've already eaten. Let's do this."

"Oh, I'm sorry, Momma. I can't do it today. Gotta make sure to catch the bus."

"What do you mean you can't do it today? It's Election Day. This is what we do. We vote. Plus, I need your help with the boys."

"I'm sorry, Ma. I just can't. I've got something important to do at school this morning."

"More important than voting? Her defiant glare—one hand on her hip and the other with a raised shoulder. "I mean, this is probably the last time we will be able to go to the polls together as a family. You are going to be graduating soon, and then you will be off at college--hopefully voting."

"Mm, I just can't. I gotta go. Maybe we can go after school today? I don't have practice."

"I have to work this afternoon and the boys have play practice. Your Aunt Joyce is picking them up after school to babysit."

"But, Ma!"

"JUST GO! Go then!" Her words cut deep. I understand why she feels the way she does and, ordinarily, I would not miss this family tradition for the world, but I have an appointment with Jolene. Of course, if I told mom what I really had planned, she would freak! I'm not ready to die, so I will just slide out the door for my date with destiny.

Standing at the bus stop, I could barely breathe with anticipation—or, it was just that cold? I kept looking down the road. Please hurry up! When I saw the shape of the bus, my teeth chattered into a slight grin.

"Morning, Jeff," I greeted the bus driver like we were old friends. Jolene may have been watching, so I wanted to appear a "man of the people." "It sure is cold out there." I breathed into my hands. I turned and looked back. There... directly in the center... she was there. The seat next to her was empty. I couldn't help but imagine others trying to claim the space, but she undoubtedly told them "Sorry, it is saved." "Reserved." "Occupied."

I made my way back to her. I had to stretch over a couple backpacks in the aisle. The bus started with a jolt as I was mid-stretch. I couldn't fall in front of her, so I managed to do some parkour, capoeira-style moves until I could aright myself. I quickly steadied enough to sit down in the row with her.

"Nice moves." Her voice soothed the awkwardness.

Embarrassed out of my skin, I still swagged, "I do my best." Masculinity validated, I could fess up, "I am sorry about last night. Coach was having a fit on the entire team about grades. He made us run suicides." I mimicked Coach's gruff, "You are gonna run until somebody pukes then we are going to run some more." We? I didn't see him run an inch." My hands were so cold, so I started rubbing them together to create some heat.

Jolene grabbed my hands. "Here, let me warm those for

you." Her warm and gentle touch could melt sugar. She rubbed and I oozed. "My name is Jolene Young. You are Na-HIM Lightbourne. Did I say that right?"

Chuckling, "Close. It's pronounced NaHEEM." The softness of her hands let me know she had mercy in her soul. She plied and kneaded the skin and muscles. Strong girl. Could it be a sign of what is to come?

"Nice to meet you. Ooh... thank you. That's much better now. So, tell me about yourself. I know you are an excellent hand warmer, but tell me more."

"Well, I just moved here after my dad was transferred for work. He's a pastor."

"Oh, yeah?" I faked not knowing. I hoped I could mask my excitement as I recalled my earlier thoughts and "bad intentions" as Camille called them.

"I used to go to the Trinity School. You ever hear of it?"

"Nope. Can't say that I have. Is it a good school?"

"I think so. I got pretty good grades there. I heard the classes are tough here. I hope I can keep up."

"What grade are you in?"

"Tenth."

"What teachers do you have?"

"Hudson for geometry. Carangi—is that how you say it? For advanced placement bio and Panella for English."

"Oh, Panella is nuts! But don't you worry about that. I got your back. He's a fanatic about note cards for research papers. He is a stickler for the rules he sets. As long as you follow his formatting on your papers, you'll be fine. I have had him before. He has a form template he puts on top of each page. Any bit of text outside of his margins is a cardinal sin. I can tutor you if you would like. Carangi is a softie. He pretends to be a hard ass, but he's a real teddy bear. Someday, remind me to tell you the story of when he caught me cheating on my research project."

"What happened? Tell me."

"Not yet. We are just meeting, and I don't want you to get the wrong idea about me. I'm no cheater."

"Tell me...." Her whine was so cute— oddly scintillating.

"Well, in tenth grade, we had to design our own research projects. I decided to test the effects of aspirin on the reproductive cycle of Drosophilae [flexing my brain muscles]—fruit flies. I had heard so often in the movies when women did not want to have sex, they would cry out 'I have a headache' so I wanted to test to see if different types of aspirin would have any effect on the reproductive rate of the flies. I was supposed to do weekly checks on the population by counting the number of egg sacs in the growth medium. I got tired of doing that, so instead of counting, I started fudging the numbers. I forgot to pay attention to the scientific birth rate. Carangi knew my numbers were wrong. He tried to rip me a new one."

"Uh, Nahim? That's cheating. You are a cheater."

"I did not cheat. I fudged. It is different" I hedged--convinced of my position. Jolene chuckled. *I like this girl.* It seemed odd and "too soon," but I reached out to take her hand to hold and she held it! So, there we were holding on to each other and we had just officially met a few minutes prior. I think we each sensed the significance of the moment because we both peeked at each other secretly from the corners of our eyes. When my look caught hers, I giggled like "Shy Brother" from The Five Heartbeats.

"Remind me to tell you about the time I planned a project to study the effects of adding iodine to growth rate of tadpoles. Oh, what a mess."

Pretty soon, the bus pulled up to the front of the school and I groaned that we would have to go our separate ways. I prepared to stand up, but her grasp tightened, and she stiffened for me to sit back down. I grabbed her hand with both of mine. She did the same.

"Nahim, I like you, but I need you to understand something. I am a Christian and I am serious about maintaining my purity. This (she held up our hands) is as far as it is going to go between us. Can you handle that?"

What else could I say? "Of course." I found the words, but the words coming out of my face were a lie. Smiling, I looked up into her smoldering eyes, "Lead and I will follow." I grinned. I have a girlfriend. I think.

Camille and Tuck were making out on my locker when I got

there. They were getting it pretty hot and heavy. "Oh, c'mon, guys. Can I get in my locker please?"

"Jealous much?" Tuck was such an ass.

"How did the convo go last night?"

"It didn't. Practice ran too late. I did not get off the bus until nearly seven thirty."

"Why didn't you call her from the bus, idiot? You were on there for like an hour."

"True. I didn't even think of that." I lowered my head for being a doofus.

"I'm so gonna win." Tuck whispered under his breath.

"But we did chat this morning on the bus. I think we're 'talking' now."

At the same time, they both asked, "You think?"

"Yeah, we held hands too."

Tucker lightly punched my shoulder. "You held hands, Go 'head, buddy. You are on your way."

"I'm not so sure. We held hands, yes, but then she played the "Christian card."

"Christian? That's the death card. You are done, dude."

"Give me some time to work my magic. I am not tapping out yet. Jesus loves her and so will I."

Chapter 7

"Baby, I want you to remember some key principles when it comes to maintaining your purity: number one: hugging leads to kissing. Number two: kissing leads to sucking. And the big one, number three: sucking leads to fu..."

"Dad!" Jolene cringed.

Never one to mince words, Reverend John Young has been told he has no filter. His more conservative parishes have been concerned that he was a little bit caustic in some of his presentation. For a long time, he has been considered a "fire and brimstone" hell fury kind of preacher.

"Okay, but you get what I am saying." No one escaped his piety, especially his daughter, Jolene. He maintained a tight leash on her and has had no problem tightening the reins if she seemed to take steps in the wrong direction. "It's not that I am worried about you going over the line, but I want you to understand you can still get burned by getting too close to the line. Your best bet is to stay away from the line altogether."

"Daddy, why don't you trust me?" Jolene pleaded for understanding.

"I trust you, honey; it's boys that I don't trust—teen boys especially. Things happen too quickly. If you don't keep your guard up, you can easily get caught up. And what do I always say, 'If you give the devil an inch, he will take a mile. If you give him a rope...'"

"He will want to be a cowboy. Dad, I've heard this speech a thousand times."

"And you can expect to hear it a few more thousand times."

"I am not going to do anything wrong. I just want to hang out."

"Hanging out doing what? Why are Christian teens always wanting to 'hang out' with non-Christians?"

"Dad, isn't it possible that I can witness to my unsaved

friends while we are hanging out?

"Probable...eh. Possible...yes. Likely? Doubtful. Isn't it a more powerful testimony of God's power that you can stay out of the Devil's territory? That you can be separate— 'in the world, but not 'of it.' What does First Peter two nine say?"

"Ugh... First Peter two nine:" Jolene recited mechanically, 'But you are a chosen people, a royal priesthood, a holy nation, God's special possession, that you may declare the praises of him who called you out of darkness into his wonderful light. First Peter two nine."

'   That's right. 'A holy nation, a peculiar people.'"

"Dad, I get that He wants us to be holy, but why weird?"

"Weird? Why do you say that?"

"Peculiar means weird, different, strange. I am a PK. I've always been considered weird and different. I just want to be normal."

"Normal is overrated. He wants us to be set apart, distinguished, unique. Peculiar in this sense basically means that as a Christian you are exempt from the ordinary pressures unsaved teens feel. You are special."

"I think the word you are looking for is boring."

"And that is why a lot of Christian teens struggle with maintaining holiness. When you consider righteous living a task, a chore, or something heavy weighing you down, there is a problem. The Bible describes salvation as a 'treasure in earthen vessels.' You are a treasure. My baby. It is my job to protect you." He reached out for a hug.

"Protect. Not smother."

"Watch your tone, young lady."

"Dad, everyone believes you're anti-dating--that you will never allow me to date anyone."

Chuckling, "I am not anti-dating. I am anti-pursuing immature relationships that bring emotional pain. First Corinthians 7:32 tells us "But I would have you without carefulness. He that is unmarried careth for the things that belong to the Lord, how he may please the Lord."

"Argh...I do not need a sermon right now. Can't you be my

dad and not my pastor?" She folded her arms in defiant opposition.

"Well, honey, your dad is your pastor. I don't know how to be anything else."

A tear fell from the corner of her eye. "I just want a boyfriend. Is that too much to ask?"

"For what purpose? Do you think you are going to marry this 'boyfriend'? What do you need a boyfriend for?"

In a begging tone, "I just want someone to like me."

"Well, I like you. Isn't that enough?'

"You are my dad. Is it so much to have a boy like me that is not my dad?"

Setting straight up to address her, " That is exactly how the enemy gets you. He puts a lure out that— a boy— to make you feel whole. But, don't you understand, you were designed to only be whole in God? With God? You do not need to date someone for that." It was his matter-of-factness that she despised.

"Isn't non-dating 'unhuman'?"

"That is not even a word, so I know you are wrong there. God doesn't want us running around chasing fulfillment. He wants our focus to be on him. If you start dating someone, the likelihood of the relationship lasting until you get married is slim to none. I want to save you from years of regret. I watch teens down at the church go from relationship to relationship. One week they are so 'in love' and the next week they are barely talking to each other. My hope for you is that you enter your marriage relationship without having to compare your husband to a long line of boys."

"Dad, it is just one boy." Immediately, she knew she let the cat out of the bag. There is no going back now.

"Oh, so now we are getting to it. We are not talking about boys. We are talking about one specific boy, right? Not just any friend that is a boy. But a boyfriend. Who is this boy?" he challenged.

"Just a boy I met in school. He is cute and nice and plays basketball."

"Great. A jock. They're the worst. He's probably so full of himself, too."

"He is also really smart. Like really smart. He has even offered to tutor me and show me the ropes around school. He's been showing me around the school and helping me with meeting new friends and calming me down when I get nervous at lunch or something."

"So, you like him."

"He likes me, so I like him."

That is the kind of nonchalant relationship with no meaning that I am trying to teach you how to avoid. It is unnecessary."

"Dad, ever since mom died, you will not let me have any freedom to make my own decisions. You are so strict. All of my friends at the church call you the Reverend Warden. Did you know that? They say it is like I live in a jail."

"And what do you say when they call me that? We accept the words people speak into our lives. Your friends do not define me, and I had hoped they do not define you. I refuse to be burdened down by the thoughts and expectations of what others say and do. I only get one chance to do this parenting thing, and when I stand before God, I want Him to say, 'Well done.' I am what God says I am. If that makes me a warden, then so be it. I am raising you by a different system than everyone else. It is up to you to embrace the values I have taught you."

Why bother? He is never going to bend. Jolene huffed upwards at her bangs.

"Your generation sees love as some kind of game. Y'all have sex before you know each other's favorite color. Love is what your mother and I had. We barely dated. If you think I'm strict, you should have seen your grandfather's rules. He was no joke. Your mom and I had a deeply committed relationship. I only kissed her lip-to-lip at the altar on our wedding day. Most of the time, I kissed her on the cheek. That was it. And I was madly in love with her. On our wedding night, her body was brand new to me. When we bought our first house before we got married, I lived in the house the first six months by myself. Can you believe I refused to sleep on our bed in our bedroom until we could join together the first time in our bed? I loved her that much." He paused before continuing, "Love is more than just a feeling. I think your life, your heart, your soul is more important than that. I don't want you to just have fleeting love. I want you to know intimacy. What your mother and I had." Grabbing his daughter's chin and cheek, "Listen, baby, holiness is right and will always be right. You need to read *I Kissed Dating Goodbye.* I'll order one for myself and one for you. Let's read it together." Rev. Young leaned over and shoulder bumped his daughter. "You and me, huh, kid? OK?

Jolene smiled and leaned in to her dad.

Chapter 8

"Dr. Davis, how did you know my dad?" Ever since he mentioned that fact on the first day of school, I wanted to know more. I did not know much about my dad—I was so young when he left. Maybe Doctor Davis could fill in some of my mental gaps?

"Aww, man! Monarch and I used to run together back in Brooklyn. We came up through school together. He was my hero. I really looked up to that dude. He didn't take any sh... uhm, stuff! And he was popular too, especially with the ladies. He had a different girl for each day of the week. He was the mack!" This trip down memory lane definitely made Doctor Davis excited. I had never seen him smile so hard. He was practically cheesing as he told me how my dad used to "chase skirts' and "chase tail." I will readily admit, Davis' stories were having the exact opposite effect on me.

"Old habits die hard, Doc."

"Oh, I am sorry, son. I should not be so crass about our exploits. Besides, that is all in the past now. At least it is for me." I don't know how or why I had told him that my mom and dad split up because of his cheating. I was just naturally drawn to Dr. Davis. I had never had a black teacher before—even when I went to school in the 'hood. I never would have expected to meet my first way out here at Hilton.

He had already opened so much of the world to me—at least, my American world. He was teaching the black presence in American as contributors not slaves. He told us about black inventions, black inventors, black excellence. He emphasized we were more than entertainers and athletes. He made us read chapters of *Before the Mayflower: A History of the Negro in America, 1619-1962*. Davis taught us how that the black narrative had been co-opted as we have been taught blackness to understand that the primary narrative within the dominant culture is one focused on tragedy and racial trauma. He supported the notion that blackness is intersectional and difficult to situate within any particular context and fits within a larger diaspora of influences. We shared presentations of success that are more of a celebration of black prosperity. We took seriously the notion that popular culture is a means to explore society and explain the racial phenomenon. He expected a focus on protests and unrest, slavery and colonization, but also black girl magic, and black boy joy–and other monikers suggesting a joyful experience. He wanted to honor a 24/7 black experience!

He constantly referred to "setting the record straight" about who really settled the land we call America. When he talked about the history of the slaves, he did so in such a way that I was no longer ashamed to be black in this white space. He taught me to feel a sense of pride when I referred to the men and women who survived despite the "brutal systems of degradation and racism" that was meant to destroy them. When he showed that picture of the slave with his back all bruised up from being beaten, I did not try to avert my gaze. I looked straight on—defiant to let these white people see they would not break me either.

In a recent class, he asked the students to define culture. People suggested "food," "clothing," "art and music," and "dance." Dr. Davis added that all of those were elements of what he called "folk culture" or what remains on the surface. Davis instructed, "Culture is a group's total way of life." He said, "the word culture comes from the Latin word colore which means 'To honor, to cultivate, and to inhabit.'" He made sure to tip my head up from my chin when he said the word "honor." I loved how the white folks did not say diddly-squat when he was teaching. It was really interesting to watch them get mad when they asked, "Why have we never been taught this stuff before?"

"It has been hidden in plain sight. All you would ever have to do is open a book. There is plenty written out there. It's even in some of the textbooks you've been reading. Sometimes, you just have to read a little deeper." He had assigned us to read a portion of *The Narrative of the Life of Frederick Douglass.* In the second chapter, Douglass specifically addresses slaves' living conditions and the misnomer that suggests that slaves were happy in bondage. Davis highlighted Douglass' argument that people misunderstood the slaves' singing as a sign of contentment when their songs were really reflecting the sadness in their hearts. We closed the session by listening to Public Enemy's epic anthem "Fight the Power" and talking about voting rights. To hear that bass being played in these grand halls was titillating. I bounced my head to the rhythm as the song played.

It was that song playing in my speakers on Saturday morning when moms busted in and said she wanted me to help her carry the bags to the Laundromat. "Aww, mom. It is Saturday! It's my only day to relax." I rolled over to cover my head with my pillow to block out the sunlight.

"Boy, you can relax when you are grown and on your own. I am up. Your lazy butt needs to be up too."

"Ma, I am tired! I just want to sleep!"

"I am tired, too. I had to work a double shift yesterday, but I don't get to call in sleepy, do I? I wish we were so well off that I could just take a short break from working. I'm tired on so many levels. There are chores that need to be done, and, I need some help around here. You got fifteen minutes to be ready to go. Brush your teeth and let's go. I don't want to be there all day. The larger machines get taken up early. The sooner we get there, the sooner we can get back." She gruffed and walked out the door.

I put on my Adidas track suit and pulled my socks up my calves. The muscles in my legs were really starting to pop. I got my dad's side of the family's chicken legs--genetics— but all the games and practices were starting to improve my physique. I was feeling my look for the day. I was glad not to have to put on that school uniform. I could just be normal—fresh and fly. Mom's head scarf and ratty clothes really brought me down though. When I complained about her look, she made sure to remind, "You don't worry about how I look. You are a reflection of me—not the other way around. Besides, why do I need to put on good clothes to go to the laundromat. Ain't nobody else in there thinking about or studdin' you and me."

We carried the laundry bags—five of them between the two of us the two city blocks to the laundromat. Once inside, momma set the bags down and went to the change machine and got quarters. I should have known it was going to be an all-day affair when she pulled out two twenty-dollar bills and changed them. The numerous clinks of dropping coins told me that my Saturday plans were ruined— even though I did not really have any plans. I just did not plan to be sitting in this spot all day. The PlayStation was calling my name.

Only two old white ladies were using the machines. At least, I think they were using the machines. They were just sitting there jaw jackin'. You ain't got no better place to talk than the laundromat? I'm sure the old folks' home has a coffee klatch y'all can be a part of. You don't have to watch people wash their dirty drawers! They were there for about forty-five minutes and when I looked over to where they had been sitting, they were gone, but soon, the place was buzzing with people.

I was taking a load out of the washer when I looked over and saw my boy AC's girl on the bench with some other dude. I don't think she saw me, but I was surely gonna keep my eye on the happenings over there. I slid over to the dryers on the sly. I peered over the machines and old girl was all up in homeboy's grill smilin' and stuff. What's up with that? If something goes down, I'm telling AC. She ain't right. I imagined having to tell him. "Yo, AC, your girl is dirty. She down here at the laundromat all booed up with some white dude. She all up in his face showing him pics on her phone and stuff. She's foul, dude."

"Nahim, get those clothes out that other washing machine over there." Mom's instructions broke the drama playing in my mind.

"Yes ma'am." Dang, she's messing up my detective mode. I walked back to the other side and dude turned around and spoke to me like he knew me. What a sweet voice. Oh wait, that's a woman. She looked like a dude; I swear. She had real short hair and an armband on her forearm. Just then, Nicole, turned around and saw me.

"Hey, 'Heem."

"Hey, Nic. How you been?" Slightly embarrassed, I dispatched the clothes in the washer to the laundry basket and took them over to where momma was waiting to put coins in the dryer.

I went back to the other side and Nicole was still sitting there.

"Yo, that's your moms?" I had forgotten Nicole was mixed. I had never seen her mother. I know her dad and he's black. They weren't there much longer.

Soon, two more white women came in. They had a little girl trailing along with them. She had to be about two or three years old. The ladies immediately began sorting and stuffing clothing into available washers. The little girl may as well have been invisible because they acted like they couldn't see her any-more. She toddled and ran around the whole laundromat with no supervision. At one point, she was even playing in the garbage can. The laundromat had a little kids' play area and the girl toyed with some of the blocks and dolls. She picked up one baby doll and started kissing it and stroking its hair. All I could think about was how many other children had done something similar and how germy that doll must have been.

The little girl talked—if you can call her blurts talking—the only words I could make out were "Happy Meal" and "Mimi." She referred to the older lady as "Mimi." I assumed it meant "Grand-ma." I call my grandmother "Mom Mom."

She went back to playing and running around. At one point she neared the table where I was folding, and I thought to myself This is how white kids keep getting stolen. Pay attention to this child, Mimi.

They were still at the washers when Momma and I folded our last batches of clothes and put them in the plastic green bags we purchased from the vending machine where those tiny boxes of detergents were stored.

Chapter 9

We returned from Spring Break on Monday, April 13th. We walked into Dr. Davis' classroom and he stood at the front of the class--his jaws tight. His arms folded; his muscular biceps strained against the V-neck sweater he wore. His wooden bow tie seemed to be cutting off the circulation in his neck. His face appeared strained. Once the students were all seated and the bell had rung, his voice boomed against the unusual silence that had fallen across the room.

"Class, you may have heard. Yesterday, Freddie Gray, a twenty-five-year-old black man in West Baltimore was arrested for suspicious reasons. The news story alleges that Gray made eye contact with a white police officer and then began running, prompting suspicion in the police officers. When the police caught Gray, he was limping and was having difficulty catching his breath. Freddie Gray had asthma; it is said that he requested his inhaler; it was denied him. When Freddie was arrested, he was breathing and walking on his own. Seven days later, he died from severe injuries—to his spine nonetheless--received while in police custody. The official police report includes no information about any physical altercation with Gray." Looking down over his bifocals, "Yet Gray somehow died with three fractured vertebrae and a crushed voice box. Such mysterious circumstances for a young man to die."

Cries of "That's horrible" and "Not again" were heard in shocked whispers across the classroom. Barely anyone looked up from their cell phones.

I angrily interrupted, "Yes, it happened again. A white police officer or a few white police officers killed a black man in their custody. And all y'all can do is scroll on IG! Am I the only one that cares that yet another UNARMED black man is dead because of the cops?"

I shouldn't have been surprised when Westley chimed in,

"What's the big deal. He was probably doing something he didn't have any business."

"How can you be so obtuse?" Davis was clearly irritated with Westley's stupidity— as was I. "Do you have to be so insensitive? A man's life was taken."

"I'm not trying to be insensitive or obtuse—whatever that means. I really just want to understand. If he was innocent and had not committed any crimes, why did he run from the police? He was clearly guilty of something."

"How can you say that?" I yelled. "You don't even have all the facts!"

"What facts? He shouldn't have run—case closed."

"Case closed?" Davis leaned forward. Let me give you some facts. Freddie Gray should not be dead. He was unarmed and in police custody. There was no imminent danger or threat. His back was broken and his voice box crushed. That is not in the police training handbook I would guess. Doesn't anyone think this is all a bit sketchy?" I few white hands raised. I raised both hands.

Alex questioned, "The police are trained to serve and protect."

"Yeah, serve up whoopings and you better protect your ass." I was not afraid to serve up a dish of sarcasm. "All of this comes on the heels of Michael Brown and Tamir Rice. It is all out war on the black man!" It's a little bit too much.

"Those were all separate and unrelated cases. We are not talking about them; we are talking about this Gray dude." Didrik needed to shut his pie hole.

"You see them as separate instances? You have the privilege of being white. I don't have the luxury of seeing these separately. All I see is a pattern of police brutality and violence against young black men."

"Take out your notebooks. Why sugarcoat it? Race is the single toughest word in our language. It complicated life since the 1600s when it was invented."

I knew this would be good. Doc was fired up.

He passionately continued. "Let's begin with the current of division that exist today over the topic. Probably the most divisive question of the day 'Is America racist?' Answering this question requires some honesty. It is difficult to imagine a time in the US where we have not struggled with the concept of equality. The beginnings of this country detail a system of inequality towards someone. It was not just black and brown people, there was much competition even for those who were technically White. Now here we are, after claiming that everyone is equal in the eyes of the law, but yet, it's that law who continuously kills unarmed black people.

"Someday, I hope there will be real justice and accountability. Someday, I hope some jury will indict and convict one of these cops. And that day, oh what a day of rejoicing that will be! Davis clapped his hands together and rubbed them in quiet and reflective celebration. Hopefully, though, there won't be a shooting of some black person in another town somewhere in the United States. All that celebration will be a tremendous letdown for the many who desperately pray for justice. It will be hope amassed and defeated in the same day.

"There are many who question the degree to which race relations have changed. They can see the progress on so many levels in education, entertainment, and politics. And, we have come far. Sure, we have twice elected a black president but how long will we be forced to see the callousness of society and the sadness of lost hope? It's easy to update a Facebook post with a MLK quote, but it's another thing to actualize those words.

"Say it, Doc." I called out with Sunday morning exuberance.

"Ugh..."

"Ugh...what, Didrik? Do you have a problem with facing the truth? There is implicit bias in the police enforcement of black men. Why is it that white male terrorists can cause massacres and still be taken alive? Like that guy in Aurora, Colorado who shot up an entire movie theater full of people? Police arrested him—no broken back. No gunshots. Maybe being white and male is the real problem?"

Some female semi-whispered an exasperated "Are you serious?"

"How many of you have seen Spike Lee's movie Do the

Right Thing?"

A couple of hands shot up amid sounds of praise "That was dope!" A few kids slapped each other high fives declaring how good the movie was.

The primary site of most of the film's racial antagonism is Sal's Pizzeria, a local neighborhood eatery where Mookie (Spike Lee) works as a delivery-man. Sal's is run by Sal and his two sons Pino and Vito. Early in the film's action, the audience meets Buggin' Out (Giancarlo Esposito), a black radical who is bothered by the fact that there are 'no brothers on the wall' (referring to Sal's 'Wall of Fame' of photographs of Italian American celebrities). Sal responds that if Buggin' Out wants blacks pictured on the wall, he should get his own business, and then he can 'put your brothers and uncles, nieces and nephews, your stepfather, stepmother, whoever you want'. Ignoring Buggin' Out's plea for representation, Sal continues, 'This is my pizzeria. American Italians on the wall only.' Buggin' Out retorts, 'Yeah, that might be fine, Sal, but you own this. Rarely do I see any American Italians eating in here. All I see is black folks. Since we spend much money here, we do have some say.'

Bothered, Sal asks, 'You looking for trouble? Are you a troublemaker, is that what you are?' Buggin' Out fires back, 'Yeah, I'm a troublemaker. I'm making trouble.' Sal grabs a baseball bat and threatens, 'You're always coming in here looking for trouble, aren't you?' He asks, 'Suppose I busted your head. How would you...?' As he approaches Buggin' Out with the bat, his son Pino grabs the bat; Sal responds by demanding Buggin' Out leave. Incredulous, Buggin' Out returns to his original argument for racial representatives and begins to list likely candidates: 'You know, Malcolm X, Nelson Mandela, Michael Jordan... tomorrow!' As Buggin' Out leaves, he calls for a boycott of Sal's Pizzeria. Sal snarks, 'Yeah, I got your boycott swinging."

"You may also recall this scene. Pino and Sal both try to get Mookie off the phone. Once Mookie is finished, Pino complains to his father that Mookie is causing the business to lose money. Pino questions, 'Why are niggers so stupid?' Mookie retorts, 'If you see a nigger, kick his ass.' Fed up, Mookie furthers the exchange with Pino:

Mookie: Can I talk to you for a second? (Pause) Who's your favorite basketball player?
Pino: Magic Johnson.
Mookie: Who's your favorite movie star?
Pino: Eddie Murphy.
Mookie: Who's you're favorite rock star? (Mookie answers) Prince. You're a Prince freak.
Pino: (Disagreeing) Boss. Bruce.
Mookie: Prince. Pino, all you ever talk about is nigger this and nigger that. All your favorite people are so called niggers.
Pino: It's different. Magic, Eddie, Prince...are not niggers. I mean, they're not black. I mean – let me explain myself. They're not really black. I mean, they're black, but not really. They're more than black. It's different.
Mookie: It's different?
Pino: Yeah. To me, it's different.
Mookie: Pino, deep down you wish you were black.
Pino: Get the fuck outta here.
Mookie: Your hair's kinkier than mine. What does that mean? And you know what they say about dark Italians?
Pino: You know, I been listening and reading – I've been reading about your leaders: Reverend Al 'Mr. Do' Sharp- ton, Jesse 'Keep Hope Alive'...
Mookie: That's fucked up. Pino: (Mimicking Jesse Jackson) 'Keep Hope Alive'. Mookie: That's fucked up. Don't talk about Jesse.
Pino: And even the other guy. What's his name? Faraman, Faira- kan?
Mookie: Minister Farrakhan.
Pino: Right. Sorry. Minister Farrakhan. Anyway, Minister Far- rakhan always talks about the so-called day when the black man will rise. What does he say? 'We will one day rule the earth as we did in our glorious past'? What past you talking about? What did I miss?
Mookie: We started civilization.
Pino: Man, keep dreaming. Then you woke up!
Mookie: Pino, fuck you! Fuck your fucking pizza, and fuck Frank Sinatra!

Pino: Yeah? Well fuck you too and fuck Michael Jackson.

"Everybody wants to praise blackness, but nobody wants to feel black. We'll pick up this discussion tomorrow. I want you to think deeply about what we've said here."

At the end of class, students filed out of the classroom in the usual fashion. I could definitely tell they were feeling some kind of way. So was I, but probably not the same feeling.

The next morning, Headmaster Williams made his usual announcements. Before his message concluded, he declared, "In light of the goings-on in Baltimore, there will be a special parent meeting tonight in Ainsley Hall at seven o'clock. We want to assure our parents that the recent discussions of racism and anti-police sentiment are not what we are about here at Hilton Prep."

I could tell by his pronouncement that his message was directed at Dr. Davis' comments in class. After class, I went to make sure he was okay.

"Doc, I heard Headmaster Williams' announcement this morning about the special meeting. You alright?"

"He called me into his office this morning and said he had gotten several complaints from parents that I called the students racists and that white men were terrorists."

"But, that's not what you said at all."

"I know that, and you know that. Somebody's dad is a big wig in the police department and got his breeches all in a bunch. Apparently, I offended some big donors and this meeting is all meant to keep the money train flowing. They are more concerned with appeasing these rich white folks than they are with a dead black man."

"Do you know if the meeting is open to students or is it just for parents?"

"I think it is open for both."

"Well, then I am coming. I will bring my mom."

When we got back to the school, the meeting had already started. Dr. Davis and Mister Williams were seated on the stage in front of a sea of white folk. Trying to enter without arousing looks, we just slid into the back row. Mom looked at the stage and leaned over to me, "What is Zeke doing here?"

I whispered, "Who is Zeke?"

"Him, that black man up there." She pointed at Dr. Davis.

"That's Doctor Davis, my American Studies teacher. He is why we are here tonight. His comments about the Freddie Gray situation stirred up a hornet's nest." Zeke?

"That is your daddy's old running buddy from back in the day. You didn't tell me that he was your teacher.
Just then, a distinguished looking white man went to the microphone. "I send my son to this school to be educated not indoctrinated. Politics have no place in the school. Why do we have to even talk about this mess?"

Davis piped in, "We've all seen how his 'let's not talk about it' plan works out. I am hopeful that we will all be able to reset our perspectives and talk openly, learn from each other, and grow stronger together."

Another white man stood to address the stage. His face was redder than a hot lobster. "If Obama was sharing this message rather than 'America has racism in its DNA' we would be having a much more substantive dialogue focusing on the real root cause---culture."

Davis wondered aloud "How do we move on to heal the American problem of the color line if we refuse to accept that racism is coded into the American framework? How can we fix what is broken without acknowledging the true problem?"

Tell 'em, Doc! In my heart I raised a Black Power fist. That would probably cause more harm than good though if I assented for real.

That statement did cause quite a stir around the auditorium. The red man added, "I have a fundamental disagreement---it's not a racism issue; it's a cultural issue. And you're right--can't fix it unless you treat the right illness."

"Cultural issue, yes. Racism is a fact of American culture requiring us to admit the darker side of this freedom and equality thing. Why argue when you're not willing or ready to acknowledge the system that created the problems you list. I don't make the argument that everything is racism, but I will acknowledge the foundation as you call it."

They discussed more politics—neither side really hearing

the other. I could tell Doctor Davis was tiring of the issue when he pivoted back to Freddie Gray's maltreatment by the police. I faded out when Dr. Davis started lecturing on implicit bias. I came back to the convo as he detailed stats from the Department of Justice. I glanced around the room and smartphone screens lit across the auditorium in the hands of the students. Seriously?

A white man in a three-piece suit and tie stood and waited for the microphone. When it was his turn to speak, he countered Doctor Davis' definition of racism. "I watched a documentary on Jackie Robinson. He experienced racism. He was equally talented (much more talented) and he worked just as hard and according to all of the pictures they showed, he was dressed in suits, nice hat, etc. They made him travel separately from the team; shower separately from the team. He experienced racism—not all of this politically-correct nonsense. This is what happens when you unfairly characterize law enforcement as broadly racist the way Obama does. It's wholly appropriate to weed out the bad eggs and to broadly offer race and diversity training to ensure understanding and awareness, but to broad brush all police officers as racist is wholly inappropriate."

From across the room, a middle aged white woman perked up to share "I think the of level of danger our police put themselves in the middle of every day they go to work...I'm not sure that you can classify that any implicit bias is unwarranted, unfair or dangerous to citizens. I think it is survival."

Standing to counter all that the school representatives had been saying, one parent suggested "I do not believe that you have any statistics that show the police are doing their job poorly. Are there some who have done it poorly? Yes, but to ignore all Muslims at the airport with backpacks just to avoid profiling is dangerous and stupid."

Davis curtly countered. "Why just Muslims with backpacks? There is plenty of empirical evidence that says young white teens are more likely to shoplift. But store employees are more likely to watch the young black teens--why? Because they believe the lie the media suggests in the inherent criminality of blacks. I have heard from your own sons and daughters about the prevalence of black on black crime. Amid the grumbles of agreement, Davis continued, "Have you paused to question the commonness of 'white on white crime'? It happens on every street in every city in this country, but it's just called 'crime'. Why racialize it for black people?"

Davis paused as he rose to his feet. "Let me address the gentleman's comments. You're failing to digest what I am saying. My comments were not an indictment on policing as a whole, but when an officer shoots and kills an unarmed individual, he is effectively denying them the due process they constitutionally deserve." Several others expressed their complaints with Davis' racial dialogues.

I couldn't take it anymore and could not sit silently while they dragged my teacher, my hero, my father, my brother Doctor Davis. From the rear of the auditorium I added, "The criminals are overwhelmingly white, but the scrutiny is given to the young black and Latino kids."

Davis picked up, "Policies like stop and frisk preference whiteness and criminalize brown skin."

"YES!" I shouted accidentally. If we were in church, I would have shouted "Amen! Preach it, brother!" I sank down in my chair to try to be inconspicuous. I just tried to sink out of sight of the searching white eyes.

Davis picked up the conversation, "To the point that shooting unarmed, fleeing men is not a prevailing characteristic of police. Well, neither is blowing things up a prevailing characteristic of Muslim Americans! In the same light that it is fair to civilly address Jihadism, it is fair to address police misconduct. One just happens to be WAY more prevalent in these United States than the other."

Lobsterface dove in, "And it is also fair to say you would avoid walking down the blocks of the inner city at night with your stroller full of kids. Not because you are racist, not because everyone that resides in the inner city is a criminal, but based on characteristics established by facts, it would be unwise."

"That is laughable. Sir, I grew up in Brooklyn, New York. I have no problem walking down the street in Brooklyn at night. It's walking here at night that scares me. I'm being 100% honest

here. As a person of color, I am capable of being and have been
guilty of horizontal oppression. I don't get a pass because I am
brown. The definition of racism that requires prejudice plus power can be used on a technicality to shield me from being accused
of racism, but that does not mean I am incapable of perpetuating
a system that upholds whiteness, anti-blackness, and racist at-
titudes, values, and behavior. I am just as responsible to holding
myself accountable as I am to holding others accountable. And,
that is why I am committed to exposing your children to antiracist
practices in education."

"But blaming race won't fix these problems only perpetuate
them. This victim mentality is not productive, and it isn't a solu-
tion--it's pandering."

"We mustn't forget historically why we have such places as
'inner cities.' Blacks fled racist areas and oppression in the South
and were only given certain areas to live because of redlining.
Then President Nixon's 'get tough' approach to the supposed 'war
on drugs' turned into a memorandum of disparate treatment of
black crime versus white crime. Davis' voice exasperated, "Should
we also mention the abject poverty, crime, and low educational
achievement within the Appalachian region--the 'outer city'? Why
haven't we criticized Bush, Clinton, Bush, Reagan, Carter, Ford,
Nixon, etc. for the white-on-white crime that happens there or
anywhere else? Or is policing blacks or other racial groups President Obama's job simply because he wears extra melanin?

Mr. Williams put himself in front of Dr. Davis at the podi-
um. I think he may have passively pushed Davis. "I fear we have
let this go on for too long, and I imagine, we could go all night
without any resolution. I am asking Doctor Davis to stick to the
approved curriculum from now on and should he desire to inte-
grate current events and controversial topics in the future, he will
discuss them with me first and we will discuss the right, preferred
method to introduce it to the students. Isn't that right, Doctor
Davis?" Williams looked at Davis and nodded his head expecting
Davis to follow suit.

"Whatever you say, man." He was pissed!

Maybe the proper thing to do here is invite Reverend Young

to close us out with a community prayer. Reverend Young?"

Reverend Young poised himself and began "Gracious and Eternal God Our Father, Holy God, my Father, we offer gratitude for the ways you have blessed our school and the ways you have blessed this local community. I pray now for the leaders who govern this community and county and that they make wise and godly decisions that are always in the best interests of our children. I am glad to live in a land where we have the freedom to speak our minds. We pray for those who oppose our set of values. I pray for them to be blessed by you God and also those who are in law enforcement. Please protect them in their line of duty so that they might protect those of us who have placed our trust in them. Unite us together with a threefold strand of cords that cannot be broken. Bind up the brokenhearted and give us peace. I am so thankful for our school teachers and leaders, and we lift them up before you. Give them wisdom to lead our children in the paths of righteousness. In many ways, Lord, our community is divided, but I pray, Savior, as you did as you looked towards heaven in John's gospel account, that we would become one as you and your father are. It is in Jesus' precious name we pray, amen."

Oh, shoot. That must be Jolene's dad! My mouth dropped open.

Chapter 10

"Really, Headmaster Williams. You don't need to babysit my classroom today. I told you I'd curtail controversial topics."

"This visit has nothing to do with you. I am just keeping my promise to the parents and to the board that I would take a more "hands-on" approach with our newer teachers. Our research shows that schools that provide high levels of support for beginners will retain more and better teachers, and students will reap the rewards of a more positive and effective learning environment overall."

"So, what you are saying is, 'it is for the kids'?" [He mimicked the air quotes] Cinching his sports jacket, "Exactly."

"Right..." Davis snarked. Averting his eyes and mumbling under his breath.

The two walked into the already populated classroom. Mr. Williams posted himself in the rear of the classroom while Dr. Davis assumed his usual position at the lectern. He took roll call and collected homework assignments.

"You were serious about that Doctor Davis?" Jeff looked worried as the other students passed their papers forward.

"Why would you think otherwise, Mr. Dent?"

"I just thought with the emergency parent meeting, you weren't going to hold us to that so we could attend."

"So, am I correct in my assumption that you did not do your homework?"

"No... I mean, yes. Wait... yes you are correct that no I did not do my homework. I didn't think we had to."

Davis picked the stacks of papers from the first desk in each row. "I guess that is what you get for thinking." The other students chuckled at Jeff's error and Davis' enjoyment of it. I giggled a little, too, and turned around to see what Headmaster Williams had to say about the joke. Disapproval weighed his eyebrows.

"We were talking yesterday about the differences in how whites characterize race relations in present society versus how blacks view it. Williams leaned forward and scooched up in his seat. Today, I would like to expand that discussion. How many of you have heard of the American Dream? Thirty-five hands shot up into the air. "All of you? Good. What is it?" The once confident crowd now turned and looked at each other in bewilderment. "Nathan? Jackie? What is the American Dream?"

"America is the land of opportunity. Everyone has the right to achieve success and prosperity through hard work and determination." Jeff chimed in.

"Is that right? Everyone? Oh, that's right. The Constitution says that we all have the inalienable right to life, liberty and the pursuit of happiness. That is the American Dream, right, Mr. Williams?" All the students' heads turned towards the back simultaneously.

Williams stood up and tugged at his jacket. He looked like he was bracing for impact. "The American Dream is a national ethos of the United States, the set of ideals in which freedom includes the opportunity for prosperity and success, as well as an upward social mobility for the family and children, achieved through hard work in a society with few barriers."

Davis walked over to the computer station with a bit of a flourish. "I thought someone would say something like that." All of a sudden a match struck on the projection screen and a fire began burning through the words of what looked to be the Constitution. The words "we the people" burned in front of our eyes. As the edges of the yellowed paper scorched, a somber tune began to play. A voice began to narrate (I recognized it was Louis Gossett, Jr. from Tyler Perry's *Daddy's Little Girls*: "What happens to a dream deferred? Does it dry up like a raisin in the sun or fester like a sore and then run? Does it stink like rotten meat or crust and sugar over like a syrupy sweet? Maybe it just sags like a heavy load or does it explode?" Black and white pictures and videos of the Civil Rights Movement underscored Gossett's lyrical interpretation.

"The famed poet Langston Hughes wrote those words in 1951. What kind of dream was he talking about here? The dreams we all experience while sleeping? Daydreaming? Most definitely not, this dream has to do with conscious goals, hopes and aims for the future. One could argue he was speaking out about this notion of the 'American Dream.' This was a full twelve years before Dr. King had a dream. Davis paced with authority.

After a brief pause, he began anew. "One could argue that the dreams of both Hughes and King have not yet been realized. Some might argue that the time for dreaming is over. Maybe it is time for American to wake up?" Davis walked back over to the computer station and began punching keys on the keyboard. He was on YouTube. Soon the words "This animation was commissioned by the African American Policy Forum" appeared on a black screen. An up-tempo instrumental song began to play. The title screen read "Structural Discrimination: The Unequal Opportunity Race." An aerial shot of a track and field event appeared while fans screamed allowed. The runners had all lined up on the start. There were four or five runners—their skin colors ranged from dark to white. The closest runner was black, and he had dreads in his hair. They all assumed the runners' crouch. All at the same starting place.

The crack of a gunshot signaled the start of the race, the white runners took off while the brown and black runners were halted by stop lights that appeared magically before them. The number 1492 showed on the scoreboard behind them. As the runners waited for the stoplight and barrier, the numbers kept ascending. Soon, the words "slavery," "broken treaties," "genocide," "manifest destiny," "trail of tears," "Dred Scott," "segregation," "Japanese exclusion," and "Chinese internment" flashed towards the brown athletes. The white runners lapped the brown ones. Soon, the white runners aged and passed their batons to the next younger white runners. The baton morphed into a large cylinder with a dollar sign emblazoned on it. The brown and black runners were still at the starting line when the white runners lapped them again. This time, as the white runners passed, the words "wealth disparities" flashed on the screen. Once the timer reached 1964, the barriers disappeared from before brown runners who lit the track. It looked like the brown racers were keeping up with the white track stars, but soon, a rainstorm titled "discrimination" began to unleash rain upon the black runners while the whites pulled ahead. I glanced around at the white students in the classroom. They were agitated—some squirming in their seats.

A few small rocks and larger boulders appeared in the lanes of the black runners. "Poor schooling" explained the rocks' presence. A giant hole in the black runner's lane opened and swallowed the black man. "Underemployment" was the name of the hole. "Standardized tests" are pictured as a lake of sharks. Cages begin to fall around and capture the darker runners. These are typified as the "School to prison pipeline." When a sign identifying a rest area appears, the dreadlocked black runner is barred by "housing discrimination" at a gated community. An official stops the black runner and hands him a cup for a urine test. "Racial profiling" appears and the runner's face is disturbed and shows worry. "Shortened lifespan" appears as a brick wall for the black runner to rest at. As he rests, construction workers build one of those automated sidewalks and the white male runner is transported even while standing still. He easily glides past the white female as the words "old boy network" shows onscreen. Still images show as portraits as the white male crosses the finish line victoriously— hands raised. The video clip ends declaring "Affirmative action helps level the playing field."

Davis launched into a series of questions at the conclusion. He did not even really wait for students to answer. "What was the time referencing? What happened in 1492? What happened in 1964? Perhaps to achieve the dream, we have got to acknowledge that the race is not fair, nor has it ever been equal in this 'land of opportunity.' Thoughts?" The bell rang and the students bee-lined out of the room. I doddled in my pride." Somebody gets me. Headmaster Williams stood up. "Great job, Davis. Challenging, but not offensive. Really thought provoking. I am really impressed by your articulateness."

The next day, out of the watchful eye of the headmaster, Doctor Davis continued in his regular manner. He took attendance quickly and got to the day's content. "It goes without saying that race is a difficult concept to discuss openly. I mean, things are unnecessarily racialized." As if a light bulb went off in his head, Davis instructed, "Everybody, close your eyes. Let's play a game.

It's word association game. I'll say a word, an occupation, or some activity. I want you—without voicing aloud—to imagine the race of the person that comes to mind when you hear the term. Everybody understand?" Once everyone gave the ready, Davis counted down. "Three, two, one. Taxi driver. Concert violinist. Rich. Professor. Welfare mother. Drug addict. Drug dealer. Mathematician. Surgeon. Poor. President. Affirmative Action. Open your eyes." There were a few groans as people's eyes readjusted to the light. "Now, let's talk about what we just did. Who will be honest and say what they saw? How many of you will admit for the negative occupations or activities, you saw a person of color? The more affluent, you saw somebody white?" I ashamedly affirmed what he had said. I was surprised when some of the white kids admitted as well.

"You see? We are all prejudiced. It doesn't make you a bad person. We have all been programmed into believing certain things about others. Much of the images we see come from the media. Movies especially are a big force behind it. Even our educational systems." He walked over to his bookshelves. "Look at our textbooks. What images do they show? What story are they telling?" He flipped through the pages as if he were searching for something. Whose history is being represented? Whose experiences are being validated?"

"But wait. When you said 'affirmative action' I saw a black woman. That's not being prejudiced. That's just being right, right?" Lexie's question seemed to resonate with the other students.

"Wait. How many of you believe that?" Multiple hands raised into the air. Incredulous, Davis queried, "Where does that belief come from—Fox News?" I chuckled. "Well, Fox News is wrong." In the United States, white women are the top beneficiaries of affirmative action programs." Several students scoffed at this little factoid. "You've heard of the ERA? Equal rights for women are an affirmative action program. It is a government program designed to right a wrong through positive intentional action. The number two beneficiary is white men."

"Bullshit. Any other teacher would have challenged such negative language."

"No, Tyler. Real shit. And watch your mouth. The GI Bill? Affirmative action for white men. When soldiers came home from war, they were guaranteed jobs as reward for serving their country. Soldiers get money for college so they can get better administrative jobs rather than factory and assembly line jobs. But look at how the term has been falsely racialized."

"Wow, I never saw it that way." Didrik seemed thoughtful with these new revelations.

Davis continued. "There are more white people on the welfare rolls than black, but the image of the black welfare queen constantly getting a handout from the government is what we see in the media. Look at the immigration debate. We hear immigration, we imagine 'those' brown people coming to steal our jobs. What jobs? Landscapers. Maids. Farmers. Meat packing plants? How many of you dream to do those types of jobs?" Nary a hand raised. "So what jobs are they stealing from whom? Has anyone ever seen *A Day Without a Mexican*? The movie imagines what life would be like for Americans if we somehow woke up to a world without Mexicans. Imagine how your life would be impacted without your servants and your nannies." He's not talking about me.

Chapter 11

"Come on, baby, send me something good. You show me yours; I'll show you mine" Nahim begged.

In her mind, Jolene got an attitude. It had been several days since they'd hooked up, and she was getting pretty tired of his constant pressure.

"Babe, no. I'm not sending you a dirty picture. I'll see you tomorrow and give you a big, sloppy wet kiss. Is that enough?"

"I just want to see your beautiful body. I think about it all the time. Just a peek to help me sleep."

"I don't want to get in trouble." She kept her eyes on the closed bedroom door. Whispering, she said, "Why are you making this so hard for me?"

"You're promising wet kisses with your sexy lips and I'm making things hard for you? Are you the pot or the kettle?" Nahim's tone was sarcastic and sensual. She knew exactly what he meant. "C'mon snap me something; it will delete in six seconds. Nothing to worry about, Jo."

"I'm going to bed. I'll see you in the morning after first period."

"I wish I was there to tuck you in. I'd give you sweet dreams."

"I bet you would, you bad boy. I love you, babe."

"Don't leave me hanging. I need to see a lil suhin' suhin'."

"And I want to hold Chocolate Thunder in my hands." She was shocked at how slutty she was becoming. "I love looking at your dark skin; it's so shiny. I'm so pasty and white. Your birthday is coming up. Can you just be patient? I promise to make it worth your while. Your 17th birthday will be plenty special. That I can guarantee."

"C'mon...hook me up. I love you sexy girl."

"Do you really? Cause I really really love you and would do anything for you. I just want us to work and stay together forever."

"Forever's a long time, girl. You're only 16. A hot, sexy 16-year-old that makes me so…mmph. I want you so bad. I'm going to have to take care of myself tonight. Give me something to help me out."

"Ugh, here!" She pulled her bra up and showed him her left breast and quickly put it away. "You happy now?"

"Naw, girl. I want more. Show me more."
She should have known the convo would go this way when he had texted her "FT3X."

Jolene really loved FaceTime, typically. It makes regular phone calls seem even more personal. It's like they're right in front of you. Like you're in the same room.

She whispered, "I'm gonna get in trouble. If my dad catches me, he'll kill me." All the while she protested, but little did Nahim know, she was already pulling down her pink sleep shorts and her panties. While they talked, she pulled out the pop socket on the back of her iPhone and had propped it up on the vanity. She undressed slowly so Nahim couldn't tell what she was doing. She kicked the shorts off, and they landed with the gold JUICY lettering facing up.

"Your dad won't find out. It's just you and me here. Your dad is too stupid to work a smartphone. Put that camera lower and let me see."

"Nahim…" She sheepishly whined.

. . . .

The news program on the television broke. In a voiceover, the anchor stated "This just in: Terrance Jackson is an 18-year-old standout student athlete at Lourdes High School in Alexander City, Louisiana. An award-winning wrestler, football and basketball player, Terrance is beloved at school and in the community. He's never been in trouble with the law a day in his life — until now. Terrance did what millions of kids in America are doing — it's called sexting--he exchanged naked text messages with a 16-year-old classmate."

The scene cuts to Nahim's mother, speaking, "First, she sent Nahim a nude video and then he sent her one in return. Why ain't she in jail too?"

The news anchor narrated offscreen. "It's an alarming statistic, but a recent study found that 54% of kids under the age of 18 have sexted before. Parents may hate it, but when it's consensual, it's definitely safer than in-person intercourse."

Ann continued, "But Terrance lives in the deep South. He's black. I'm not condoning his behavior, but it seems his biggest mistake wasn't doing what most American teens are all doing. His biggest mistake was doing it with a WHITE girl.

Breaking back in, the reporter talked "Her father called the police when they discovered what was happening. Terrance was arrested, charged with contributing to the delinquency of a minor and possession of child pornography for the video he still had of her on his phone. For the record, she's 16 and he's 17. Yes, she sent him a video first. Yes, this was consensual. They attend the same high school together.

The news story cuts to an interview with a police officer. Lt. Bill Davis, of the Alexander City police, was asked whether or not race played a role in the arrest. "It doesn't matter what your race, what your religion, what your ethnicity, don't do child pornography! Plain and simple."

The story cut away from Davis and the camera focused in on Dan Thorn. He stands straight except he's leaning a little trying to hold his earpiece. The red and white power tie screamed attention against his navy blue sportscoat. As if finishing Lt. Davis' sentence, "Except a 16-year-old and 17-year-old in the same school consensually sending each other sexual videos of themselves isn't child pornography. There are wide-ranging opinions on this matter."

Thorn continued, "In Louisiana, the law states that anyone under the age of 17 found to be sexting any person of any age can be charged with a misdemeanor. It's not widely prosecuted. If a 17-year-old, even if they are in high school together, does the very same thing, with a 16-year-old, they can be charged with child pornography. The law lacks the nuance it deserves and ultimately criminalizes common youth misbehavior between peers. Now, this young man faces the prospect of having a criminal record and his mother is having to scrape together every single dime she can find, $4,000 already, just to defend him from these outrageous charges. Back to you in the studio, Denise."

"Joining us with more on this subject is civil rights activist, Shaun King. King has been a very vocal supporter of the Black Lives Matter Movement speaking out against police brutality in the wake of the police shooting—what he calls murder—of Tamir Rice."

The camera pans to King. Although fairer skinned, King's face flushed with ire. "Yes, this is a bogus symptom of the mass criminalization of black folk in the New Jim Crow. Of course, race has everything to do with these trumped-up crimes. Millions upon millions of teenagers are doing this very thing and he was selectively targeted among them, and made an example of, because he crossed a line that clearly irritated not only her white father but white law enforcement officers as well. Y'all keep forgetting this kid is a star student, highly sought after and on his way to the Ivy Leagues. Y'all messing with his life. These charges should be dropped against this young man and his mother, a single mom of four, should be reimbursed for all of the needless expenses of this charade. Beyond that, these laws must be adjusted to have nuance for normal sexual behaviors between two consenting 16 and 17-year-old kids. And that's what they are—kids. This is a matter for the parents not the police!"

Denise returned, "We'll keep following this story and update you when we hear something new. Denise Richards, WKLA News."

"He deserves to go to jail."

"Why, Daddy? He didn't do anything that bad.

"Oh, child pornography is 'not that bad'?

"Oh, Daddy, you are so old-fashioned. Kids do that all the time." In her mind, Jolene thought about her recent phone call with Nahim.

"Really? Have you done it?"

"Oh, Dad. Eat your grapefruit."

Chapter 12

"Hey, are you on IG?" Nahim inquired.

"Well, that's a little complicated. I secretly have two accounts. My dad has been monitoring my social media since my youth pastor suggested parents be more aware of the social media their kids are using. My rinsta is @jojodancer, but if you want to follow my finsta, it's @justjojo."

"You have a finsta?" Nahim was learning all kinds of new things about his girlfriend he'd never expected. He chuckled. "Did you know that *Jo Jo Dancer* is the title of a movie about Richard Pryor's life?"

"Duh! I'm not stupid, sir. I love me some Richard Pryor! My favorite movie of all time is *Bustin' Loose*! Have you seen it? Mimicking the character from the movie, "Mr. Braxton, Mr. Braxton, Dakota gotta go pee!"

At the same time, they finished the scene, "Let the bear pee in your pocket! Leave me alone!" Nahim and Jolene burst out in laughter.

"He was so nasty. Did you hear him tell that one joke? He said, 'My father died fucking.' Jolene looked around as she whispered the rest of the joke. 'He did. My father was 57 when he died. The woman was 18. My father came and went at the same time.' She briefly paused to compose herself. "Do you think my dad, the Rev. Young, knows his only daughter loves that joke? We'll just let him think jojodancer relates to my dancing career. I took dancing lessons all my life. He'd kill me if he knew the real deal."

"Sure, he'd kill you. Every other word out of Pryor's mouth is MF."

"And that's why we don't tell the good Reverend the truth. What he doesn't know....." Jolene paused before revealing, "I only let him see the rinsta. Justjojo is where the party's at."

"What's a good, clean, wholesome girl like you know about

a finsta?"

"Don't mock me, sir, I'm saved but I got hands." Jolene playfully slapped boxed with Nahim.

The bell rang interrupting their sparring match. "Well, Imma hit you with that follow at lunch, my insta is @ballinfortheonetime." Later that day during his study hall, Nahim opened Instagram and began to follow @justjojo. His mouth dropped open when he saw Jolene's nearly naked photos in her bikini by the pool.

Chapter 13

On Saturday, Nahim had an appointment to go to Dr. Davis' house. When he arrived, the car sat in the driveway; so Nahim kept ringing the doorbell several times with no answer. He told me to come at 10. Pulling out his cell phone to verify the time. 10:00 on the button. When he had awakened this morning, Nahim dressed with purpose, gulped his breakfast, and kissed his momma before he left. He would not be late or risk disappointing his mentor—his hero.

Hearing a roaring motor coming from the rear of the house, Nahim stepped off the front porch and tipped around the side of the house being careful to take note of the colorful flowers aligning the edge of the property.

Nahim had to sidestep a bush to avoid the leafy guard. He looked up and saw the object of his mission. Nahim was so impressed as he saw Dr. Davis in normal clothes—not the fancy sport coats and bow ties he wore at school. Here at his home—off duty--home, he wore a beater and Nike slides. That dude is JACKED! Look at those biceps. Nahim's face lit up as he surveyed Davis' muscular frame. He sucked in air as he took in the sight.

"Hey, Doc." Nahim raised his voice in competition with the motor on the pressure washer Davis used on his deck.

"Oh, hey, young blood. I'm sorry. I got caught up doing my chores. What time is it?"

"10:00 on the dot. Is this a bad time? I can come back if you need me to." Nahim didn't want to be a bother. It would sure be disappointing though, to be turned away though. He didn't want to mention how difficult it had been to get all the way out to the 'burbs—two trains and three buses to be exact.

"Naw. It's the perfect time. I've been wanting to take a break anyhow. I've been in my feelings as I've been working. If you had come any earlier, you'd probably have caught me crying as I remembered the savagery of Bull Connor and his fire hoses. This thing," Davis held out the pressure hose, "is powerful." I squirted my foot with it. I thought it would take the skin off. That's when my mind wandered." Nahim perceived Davis' eyes did seem wet. "Come on in the house. Let's talk." As the two passed through the screen door, Davis put his hand on Nahim's back. "You want something to drink? I've got coffee, water. You want some orange juice?"

Nahim wanted some orange juice, but answered, "I'll just have some ice water."

Davis grabbed a glass from the cabinet and walked over to the refrigerator. Nahim inspected the house as he waited. Davis had real taste. Nahim marveled as the ice cubes and water came right of the fridge like a vending machine.

As the pair settled into their seats, Nahim twinged in nervousness. He gulped his water as his attention turned towards a shiny ice cube in the cylinder.

"Uh, Doc. Who's Bull Connor?" Nahim's ignorance made him incredibly self-conscious and ashamed in Davis' presence—in his home no less.

"You don't know who Bull Connor was?" Exasperated, Davis scolded, "I don't know what's wrong with your generation. Y'all don't know anything! I know Monarch hasn't been around because I can't imagine he'd let you walk around ignorant. I bet you know all the lyrics on the latest A$AP Rocky CD, but you don't know who Bull Connor is.

Nahim's face alighted in surprise. "Doc, you know A$AP Rocky?"

"Of course, I do. I love me some hip hop. Big L, Biggie, Nas, Dre. What have I been trying to tell you? You've got to pay attention to the world around you. I like "Everyday." I don't know why he has to call women bitches and every other word has to be 'nigger.' Why does your generation do that? That word is deplorable. You degrade yourselves every time you call each other that."

Throwing up his hands, Nahim retorted, "Doc, you're so old fashioned. We've reclaimed it. Besides, he's not saying 'niggEr,' he's saying 'niggA.' There's a difference."

"What do you mean you've reclaimed it? It was never yours to claim. That word was foisted on our people as a mark of dishon-

or. Hmph, you reclaimed it. You don't even know who Bull Connor was. Talking 'bout some 'Who's Bull Connor?' You need to learn your history.

Nahim huffed. "Doc, it ain't that serious. People your age need to let go of the past. We've taken the power away from the word. It's ours now!" Your generation needs to die off or some-thin', so we let go of some of these 'pains of the past' and move on into the future."

"You can't tell me you'd be so casual if Westley came up to you and said, 'What's up, nigga?'"

"That's different." Nahim tried to slough off the charge.

"How is it different?" Davis' demeanor and tone turned serious and the creases in his forehead tightened.

"I don't know. It just is. If Westley says it, I know he's us-ing it as an insult. If my boys use it, it's a term of endearment."

"Oh, that's nonsense. That word comes from a dark place—has ALWAYS come from a dark place. It was intentionally created to denigrate and dehumanize our entire race of people, and y'all out here using it for fun."

"I told you, Doc, we've reclaimed..."

Interrupting, Davis added, "You've 'reclaimed' it. How are you going to reclaim something that was never yours? We didn't invent that word. White people invented it. You think because rappers are slinging it around, we have somehow 'made it.' Like it doesn't matter anymore that y'all are giving white people license to call you one? You are under the false assumption that because Eminem is rapping, Justin Timberlake is singing R&B, and Usher is on the pop charts that somehow we've achieved racial harmony."

"You can't tell me you've never used that word." Nahim grasped for the upper hand.

"Sure, I have. Many of my friends have and still do. I grew up saying it, but that doesn't give me an excuse. I am from the streets of Brooklyn. Of course, I've used that word, but, with edu-cation, I've evolved."

"I just don't get why your generation takes this so far." Nahim sneered.

"Boy, it was MY generation that paved the way for you and your lil homies. So, you respect the struggle. We marched, we sat down, we stood up, some of us died--all to take the sting away from that word. So, don't you dare try to act like you're "down" and you have no clue who Bull Connor was."

"Then educate me, Teach. No disrespect. Who's Bull Connor?"

"Go read a book. Hell, Google it." He paused, "Did you know there's an old insult that says 'If you ever want to hide something from a black person, hide it in the pages of a book. Don't be that guy. Brother James Baldwin said 'Not everything that is faced can be changed; but nothing can be changed until it is faced.' Scoffing, "And If you part your lips to say 'Who is James Baldwin?', we're gonna fight. Davis's wide smile suggested he was not being serious.

The two talked for what seemed like hours. When Nahim made his exit, he did not leave empty handed nor empty-brained. Davis had given him a satchel full of reading materials—heavy books—and they had made a gentlemen's agreement to meet every two weeks to discuss one of the publications. On the bus ride home, Nahim rifled through the bookbag. The titles included *The Fire Next Time* by James Baldwin, *Invisible Man* by Ralph Ellison, *Things Fall Apart* by Chinua Achebe, and Walter Rodney's *How Europe Underdeveloped Africa.*

He saw a familiar image on one of the covers; Nahim settled back in his seat and opened The Autobiography of Malcolm X. Rapt at the opening words "Behold, America." He read Attalah Shabazz's reflections in the foreword to Alex Haley's biography of her father. He recognized Haley's name as the author of Roots, the televised slavery miniseries his mother made him sit through for six straight hours.

Nahim imagined the booklist as a syllabus for a college course on black radicalism. Never one to "read for fun," Nahim planned to take the challenge seriously. He internally pledged to make his mentor proud. Suddenly, Nahim sat up as he realized he and Davis never got to talk about the whole reason for visiting Davis at home. Dr. Davis was supposed to help him draft his personal essay for his college applications.

"Shoot!" Nahim looked around to make sure no one heard his outburst.

Chapter 14

On the bus ride home, Nahim pulled several of the titles from his bag. He was definitely drawn to the reddish orange of Baldwin's Fire Next Time. Doc Davis spoke so highly of "Brother James," Nahim knew that was the place to start.

He paged through the text. He read the liner notes with deep interest. He immediately wanted to tear into the essay "My Dungeon Shook: Letter to My Nephew on the One Hundredth Anniversary of the Emancipation." Already, the chapter spoke to much of the pain he had been feeling. He wanted to find a way to escape from about America's mission to destroy Black men.

He felt American had had it out for the Black man for a long time. Ever since he stumbled on Birth of a Nation, the feature film that set America's penchant for hating the black man—interestingly enough, all played by white men in blackface. When he later learned of the film's subtitle celebrating the rise of the Ku Klux Klan, he grew fairly assured of the racism of the country.

Nahim heard himself "Amen" when he read Baldwin's words describing America as a "innocent country" that had dropped the black man into a "ghetto, in which, it intended that you should perish."

The relatively short essay ended with the narrating uncle suggesting the emancipation [of Negroes] was "100 years too soon." Uncle James suggested "we cannot be free until they are free." That was where he would start with his mentor, Doctor Davis."

What do you think he meant by "We cannot be free until they are free?" Nahim questioned his mentor.

"Well, Brother Martin said we are all caught up in an inescapable network of mutuality. He meant my success is bound to your success. My freedom is your freedom. Our skin tone is what unites us." Doctor Davis walked over to the coffee pot and poured himself a cup of joe.

He continued, "We've got to eschew this thinking that "all my skinfolk ain't kinfolk.""

Nahim laughed, "Ha! That's real talk though! I've never heard that before. All my skinfolk ain't kinfolk."

Davis laughed too, but he was serious. "That type of thinking creates tribes, and America's racial problem cannot be tribal, the solution is national."

"Can you say more about that tribal thing?" Nahim allowed himself to be vulnerable around Davis.

"Sure, youngblood. We've got the classes—poor and rich, young and old, educated and streetwise. They never talk to each other and don't try to understand each other." Davis paused and sipped from his cup, "Forgive my rudeness. You want some coffee or something else to drink?"

Nahim wanted to feel grown up, so he answered, "Sure, I'll take some coffee with cream and sugar. Davis returned to the coffee pot and poured a cup for his protégé. He spilled a bit as he walked back to the table.

"Ooh, that's hot!" He fanned his hand to cool it off. When he reached Nahim, he handed the cup to him and said, "Let me get your cream and sugar. Is milk okay?"

Nahim had only drunk coffee once with his mother but didn't really enjoy the taste. "Yeah, milk is good."

Davis brought the gallon jug from the refrigerator. He unscrewed the top and poured a tablespoon or so into the steaming mug. He slid the sugar bowl to Nahim who spooned several heaping spoons into his brown liquid. He stirred the cup to distribute the sugar. He swigged and immediately drew a couple more scoops of sugar.

"Dang, boy. Have a little coffee with your sugar."

Nahim chuckled at the suggestion. "It's the only way to drink it."

Davis wanted to get back to business. "Let's talk about the second essay. What did you think about ""Down at the Cross: Letter from a Region in my Mind?"

"Honestly, I think it addresses your tribalism argument. Christians versus non-Christians, the saved and the unsaved. And let's not forget the Muslims being spurred on by Minister Malcolm."

Davis nodded his head in surprised agreement. "True talk. It's right there in the title 'From a Region in My Mind." Baldwin was raised in a very strict church. His father was the pastor, and he himself was being groomed for the pastorate. He sort of grew away from the church's teaching and ultimately left the church because he was gay, and his dad wasn't having it. He wrote about his journey of discovery in *Go Tell It on the Mountain*. The Muslims wanted him for their tribe. The Honorable Elijah Muhammad personally tried to recruit him. Baldwin describes how Black Muslims had. made a 'black god' to avoid the oppression of a 'white god' that Christianity has established within the Black community. And in the Black community, you don't mess with people's thought about God."

"Is that why Malcolm and MLK didn't get along?" Nahim tried to showcase his knowledge of the Civil Rights Movement.

"Where did you get that from? That's the tribal thing again. They somehow only met once. Coretta Scott King, Martin's wife, acknowledged that the two men might have had a great friendship. "I think they respected each other," she said. Sadly, a year after they met Malcolm was assassinated—by his own tribe." He whispered, "With the help of the U.S. government." He pulled from his own coffee mug.

"And I think that's the whole point of the essay. He was indicting religion for perpetuating narrow thinking, promoting separatism, and urging racial violence. The essay imagines American life without the divisions. Oh, wait, what did he say?" Nahim hurriedly reached into his backpack and flipped through pages in the text. "Oh, here it is.

If we – and I mean the relatively conscious whites and the relatively conscious blacks, who must, like lovers, insist on, or create, the consciousness of others – do not falter in our duty now, we may be able, handful that we are, to end the racial nightmare, and achieve our country, and change the history of the world."

"Ok, you're getting it now!" He grinned with that classic Davis smile. "See, you can be angry at white folks, but it's still your own responsibility to heal the land." He concluded with the thought of "without radical change, racial division and injustice will lead to a destructive, imploding future."

"Radical change, huh?" Nahim paused in contemplation.

"You're ready for college. This is the kind of stuff you'll hopefully encounter there. This is the type of philosophical discussion that makes for socially and politically engaged students. Brother Baldwin would be proud of you. Hey, I'm proud of you." He ruffled Nahim's hair.

Nahim sighed and for a moment felt a twinge of disappointment. He wanted a dad.

Chapter 15

Nahim and Dr. Davis finally worked out some time to sit down and work on Nahim's essay. Davis seemed proud of Nahim's fluency in his writing.

"Where do you want to go to college?" Davis inquired.

"I have no clue, honestly. I am going on a college tour sponsored by the guidance office. Mrs. Mastrangelo set it up. Coach Payne thinks I should be looking at Division One schools. I have been thinking about the Cavaliers at the University of Virginia. I think I would like to play there." Nahim adjusted his shirt. He always wanted to look "straight."

Davis harrumphed. "I hope ball is not the only reason you are looking at UVA."

"Doc, come on, ball is my life." Nahim proudly and sarcastically snarked.

"Well, do you at least know what you want to major in?"

"Not really." Nahim's face turned downtrodden. He did not like feeling as if he is such a disappointment to Dr. Davis. "Maybe something with Criminal Justice."

"Criminal Justice, huh? Lord knows that is an area we need good people. The system is truly f'ed-up." Davis slowed his speech rate and over pronounced his pseudo-curse word.

"When is this trip? Have you applied yet? Do you know anything about living in Charlottesville? What is it like for black kids like yourself? You know that Thomas Jefferson used slaves to build that college?" Nahim's mind raced as Dr. Davis rapid-fired questions at him. Why give your money to a slave school? Why not go to an HBCU?

"The trip is this weekend. We're leaving in two days." Nahim looked forlorn and crestfallen. He stood up from his desk to leave Davis' classroom. Davis was writing something on a sheet of paper without looking at Nahim. As Nahim lifted his backpack from the floor, Davis didn't stop writing. "Wait. I've been on these college tours before. These schools show you a bunch of glitz and glamour. They will bring you to the nicest, cleanest residence halls; have you talk with the best and the brightest students; the most wired classrooms— mere trinkets and toys." He paused while focusing his eyes on Nahim. "But, if you have seen one, you have seen them all. You need to have a plan."

"A plan?"

"Yes, a plan. You are going to see a bunch of the same dog-and-pony shows—hear a bunch of the same lies and half-truths. Yet, you will need to ask yourself one important question. One thing to keep in the front of your mind... How will you know it is the right place for you? It's easy (and perhaps tempting) to think your costs are limited to the line-item expenses—tuition, fees, room and board, and books— the admissions officers will so helpfully break down the numbers for you for you. Count the costs. What will make you happy?" Davis stood up and walked from the rear of his desk to approach Nahim. When he was within inches of his young charge, Davis reached out and grabbed Nahim's shoulders. "Think about the hidden costs--getting home to visit your mother a couple times a semester. These are things they will not tell you about." Nahim parted his lips to interrupt, but his mentor kept speaking,"

"Have you even weighed your daily living expenses— you will need about $2,000 each year for laundry, cell-phone bills, and anything else you normally spend money on. And I know you like to eat out. Pizza. Wings."

Nahim chuckled, " You got that right." Nahim reached around Dr. Davis' muscular arms to put his hands on those bulging biceps. "Man, I have got A LOT of thinking to do. You've got me messed up."

"I didn't mean to 'mess you up;' just want you to go into this with your eyes wide open. This is one of the most important decisions of your young life. I almost hate that you're going with a group. It can be so easy to get caught up in groupthink."

"Groupthink? What is that?" Nahim's face twisted in confusion.

"That is when people who experience things together start thinking alike. Let some one person not like one of the dorms. All of a sudden somehow everyone has the same problem. You almost need to visit colleges alone. You and maybe your mama."

Nahim said his goodbye to Dr. Davis. As he left the classroom, his mind flooded with all of Dr. Davis' advice and questions. He took a few steps into the corridor. He reached deep into the right pocket of his khakis and pulled out his cell phone and flipped it open. Pressing several buttons, the phone rang. After a brief moment, he heard the voice of the intended call recipient. "Hey, Ma." After a few moments, Nahim responded, "Ma, if I like the University of Virginia, will you go back and visit again with me? Ma, I told you I was going on that college tour with Mrs. Mastrangelo. It's Thursday and Friday. I know I didn't remind you, but that is because I put it on the calendar on the fridge." Voicing frustration, Nahim barked, "Ma, can we talk about all this later? Ma, I told you. We did talk about this before. Mom!" Seconds later, he slammed his phone shut. I'll probably regret that later! "Babe, what's wrong?" Jolene sensed Nahim's concerned frustration from afar as she saw him walking down the hall on his way to practice.

"I just got into it with my mom. She's trippin'. She forgot I am going on the college tour this week, and somehow that is my fault. I ended up hanging up on her. Now I am going to have to deal with that when I get home. Nahim's frown suggested emotional pain. Jolene was not sure what she should do. She grabbed Nahim's left hand and pulled him closer for a silent hug.

"Aww, babe. I am sorry. Anything I can do?" Jolene playfully rubbed Nahim's head. She wanted to reassure him that everything would be fine. From the stories Nahim had told her about how strict his mother was, Jolene doubted the offense of hanging up on his mom would not be received well.

"I've gotta run, babe. I am already late for practice. Coach will be mad." Nahim scrambled off down the hallway.

"Call me later!" Her voice intermingled with the clopping sounds of Nahim's footsteps as he galloped his down the way.

Chapter 16

The sun brightly shone through the bus window and woke up the snoring bodies who had sprawled every which-a-way on throughout the bus. Bodies lay strewn across the seats, legs crossed the aisles between seats. Some folks had even dared to crawl on the floor to find a space to stretch out to give themselves and their seatmates room. Nahim groaned while his body adjusted to its wake position. His bones creaked as he sat aright. Once his eyes had adjusted to the brightness, Nahim made sense of his surroundings. He watched out the window just as the bus drove past a road sign indicating Charlottesville was a mere 20 miles away.

Nahim had not planned to fall asleep. His intention was to stay awake the entire trip. In fact, he had surprised himself. He had never really trusted his fellow travelers, but the comfort of the bus's quiet drag lulled him into unconsciousness, especially as the others' quieted their constant chatter and the low purrs of sleep replaced words in English. After a while, there was no one to interact with amidst the darkness that had enveloped the motorcoach.

Soon, Mrs. Mastrangelo, our guidance counselor and chaperone, stood at the front of the bus next to the driver. The intercom system crackled and her voice boomed over the bus speakers. "Ugh, turn it down," I yelled from the back, "It's too early to be so loud." This statement belied the fact she could probably hear the music pouring through my Beats headphones at full blast.

"Students, we're only about ten minutes away from our destination. Let's start getting ourselves together. Wake up! Wake up! Wake up!"

One last stretch and I felt like a million bucks. I reached for my bag underneath the seat. I opened the drawstring open to obtain my hairbrush. I untied the DuRag atop my head and began to brush my hair with intention. Deep short strokes was the best way to ensure waves would appear. Each time I brushed, I smoothed my hair with the opposite hand. When I was done, I put both the DuRag and brush back into the duffle and pushed it back under the seat.

"I've asked the driver if we could make a quick pit stop at a gas station, so we could freshen up a bit," Mastrangelo's voice broke over the intercom.

"Oh, thank God. Some of y'all, Tommy, need to brush your teeth." Jackie's insult of Tommy was met with chuckles and snorts. I laughed as well, but my breath was kickin' too. I was glad for the potential stop.

Talking to her friend, Amanda questioned, "Kiera, how are you putting on lipstick before you brush your teeth?"

"There might be some cute boys at the station. Just wanna look my best."

Hmph, maybe Kiera's right? Taking her hint, I thought it a good time to look my best as well, so I reached back into my bag and pulled out a nice polo shirt I had packed for the tour. I sure am glad my mom made sure I had ironed it before I packed the bag last night. Taking it out, I was surprised the fabric survived the trip unwrinkled. I removed my T-shirt and slipped the polo over my head being careful not to muss my hair. Fresh to death. In a shocking turn, the bus soon turned into the women's locker room as young ladies began to undress and re-dress in front of each other. I was thrilled to be a spectator and was glad as I imagined white girls have no shame. I am not complaining; just making a note. I mean, sure, it was just bras, but a boy can imagine, right? I was not the only one ogling. Most of the boys were silently surveying the landscape as arms raised above the girls' heads as they changed. I did take note that Sally Walker was not among the ladies who prepped on the bus. Sally was on the plus-ser side, so she was probably ashamed to reveal herself like the slimmer girls did. The bus winded through the mountain roads. I am amazed at how the driver managed to maneuver the long coach through areas I didn't want to drive a car through. By the time the bus bulled into the Big J Travel Plaza and unloaded, most of the female students had made a radical transformation.

"We're only going to be here for about 15 minutes, so don't doddle. In and out. Brush your teeth. Use the bathroom. No shopping, no eating. We'll be having lunch on campus when we get there." Mastrangelo warned she would let the bus would depart with or without someone but everyone knew she was bluffing. Despite her wolf tickets, I immediately went to the Cinnabon kiosk which was just to the left of the entrance. Those Caramel Pecanbons are my weakness. I quickly bought one and practically swallowed it whole. I inhaled that thing. I'm not even sure I chewed—straight down my gullet it went. It was a fresh batch too. The caramel frosting was smooth and warm and it oozed throughout the layers of the dough.

I took care of my bathroom duties and returned to the bus. Standing outside were a gaggle of young girls coifs poofed, ponytails drawn up, and faces painted. Several had struck poses as camera phones flashed and zoomed in on duck lips and tooted butts. Mrs. Matrangelo pleaded for the ladies to get back on the bus rather than delay any further. "Please girls, we have an appointment at the Admissions Office at 11;00, so we need to get to campus soon, so we can have lunch before we go on the tour. The bus turned onto campus and parked next to a large brick building. "Ladies and gentlemen" Mastrangelo announced, "Welcome to the University of Virginia. This is the Observatory Hill Dining Hall. We've got about 90 minutes before we have to be at the Office of Admissions for the information session. So, why don't we spend about an hour here. It's all you can eat. Whatever you want, all that you care to eat, you can have it. Let's just go inside and I'll get us checked in. Leave your stuff here on the bus. The driver will lock the door." The students filed off the bus one at a time.

Mrs. Mastrangelo hustled to the front of the pack so she could get to the cashier first. She tried to be nice letting people walk through the held door but soon realized if she continued deferring to others, she'd lose her front position. Once she'd assumed her position, she paid for the entire group's meals. She turned to face the teen horde responding, "Millie here is going to give us the lay of the land; then we'll find some places to sit. Then we'll break up to get food. Remember, take all you want to eat. Don't be greedy or wasteful. Millie, the floor is yours." Mastrangelo signaled for Millie to take the front and center. With her diminutive frame and buxom features, Millie seemed misshapen and unbalanced as she waddled to a centralized location. Wearing a white polyester uniform bedecked with teal-colored plastic dollar store jewelry.,

Millie spoke up to address the crowd. "Folks, welcome to O-hill. As your teacher said, this is one of the main dining halls on campus. It's all you care to eat. Let me show you around a little bit." Millie broke ranks and led the group to the middle of the great room. "Here is the salad bar. It's important to eat your green vegetables." She continued, "Over to your right are the main dining stations." Gesturing toward the food line, "The farthest line is 'Home.' That's where you get your meat and potatoes kinds of food—just like home, get it. Today, it's beef, rice and fresh vegetables. The next line is the Pacific Grille where you can get your fresher, healthier options. On today's menu, we have shredded carrots, jasmine rice, tofu, sautéed red and green peppers, and steamed sugar snap peas. That one's mostly featuring vegetarian and vegan options. The final option here is the deli. Sliced turkey, a variety of cheeses, ham, tomatoes, lettuce, pickles. Ugh, what am I explaining for? I'm sure you can figure out what's available in the deli line." A few laughs echoed through the crowd. "Nevertheless, enjoy your lunch." Millie returned to her post at the front desk.

"Well, you've heard your options. We'll just take these tables right here in the center. Eat hearty. We'll eat and then we'll go over to Newcomb Hall for the Admissions presentation and campus tour. Meet me back at the bus in 45 minutes. Oh, did you guys see the drink stations off to the sides and the dessert station in the middle? I think I saw some dangerous looking chocolate chip cookies over there.

Chapter 16

"Ugh, I am so full! I think I ate too much." I rubbed my belly in satisfaction as we disembarked the bus when we pulled up to Newcomb Hall after lunch. "That was some good food. I wonder if it's like that every day?"

"I guess that's why you have to worry about the freshman 15, huh?" Mrs. Mastrangelo chuckled.

"I've heard about that. That's where you gain fifteen pounds as a freshman, right? Eating all that institutional food. It's no wonder. All-you-can-eat for three meals a day. I hope this admissions thing isn't boring. It might have my –itis acting up. I'll be in here dead asleep."

"We've come a long way for you to be in here sleep, Nahim. Maybe you can control yourself, huh?"

"We're here for two days, Mrs. M., I am sure I'll get the idea." I poked my chest out with confidence.

Mastrangelo stopped at the steps leading to the entrance. She turned to the crowd. "Students, when we go in here, we're going to hear from an admissions representative. I expect that you're all going to be alert, respectful;, and on your best behavior. Remember, you're representing yourselves, Hilton Prep Academy, your parents, the board, and the people who helped organize this trip." She enumerated on her fingers each organizer she mentioned. "Now let's go in." She removed a small clipboard from her purse. When we're done here, we'll likely be going on a tour of the campus. We'll then have some free time to explore on your own. We'll meet up later to go to dinner. We're going to explore using the buddy system so no one gets lost." She read from her pad the arbitrary pairings. I could tell the pairings were made alphabetically when she announced, Lightbourne, Lopresti. I looked up to realize I had been partnered with Antonio Lopresti, a known miscreant and troublemaker.

"Aw, come on, Mrs. M. Lopresti?

"You'll be good for him, Nahim. Set a good example, huh.
"Whatever you say." I gruffed.

Once the mates were paired, Mastrangelo signaled for us to walk the stairs to the admissions auditorium.

We found the auditorium and filed into our seats. Lopresti sat right next to me. I leaned towards him and whispered, "I hope this is good."

Shortly thereafter, the lights slowly dimmed and a video began on the screen in front of us. Fog hovered over a range of mountains during sunrise. It was quite reminiscent of the bus ride from the interstate to the campus. A drone took an aerial video of what I assumed was the campus. It looked like a small farm on a rural countryside from three or four hundred feet except for the one building with the rounded roof.

Soon a narrator's voice boomed about the "pulse of the university" as scenes of students around fire pits, playing Frisbee, and other activities scrolled by. Student narrators began talking about UVA being a "home away from home" and "finding your place'. I started getting angry as I noticed no black students in any of the scenes talking about community. None in the classroom scenes either. I was totally prepared to write off UVA. In my head, I screamed "Where all the niggers at?" Not one appeared until they started talking about athletics on campus. Then they were everywhere holding balls and trophies. Dr. Davis was right. I'm glad he made me read *The New Plantation: Black Athletes, College Sports, and Predominantly White NCAA Institutions*.

The author made the case solid by arguing the parallels between colonialism, the American slave system, and the structure of the athletic-industrial complex, he makes a powerful case that America's predominantly white universities give far greater priority to exploiting the bodies of black male athletes than to developing their minds. The book exactly what was being displayed in front of me: the only thing black folks can do on a white campus is prove their physical prowess not their intellectual power. At that, I decided against the University of Virginia and my mind drifted to that scene in Spike Lee's Do the Right Thing where Mookie and Pino traded racial epithets. Pino told the UVA story plainly as he described blacks as "You gold teeth, gold chain wearing, fried chicken and biscuit eating monkey, ape, baboon, big thigh, fast running, high jumping, spear chucking 360 degree basketball dunking titsoon spade moulinyan. Take your fucking piece of pizza and go the fuck back to Africa." As it did when I watched the movie years ago, The absence of black folks from this campus footage pissed me off. No black folks, really? Oh wait, there's one. A black professor wearing a greyish blue suit sitting alone with students on some couches. Here he is sharing the importance of being a part of an institution that values outside the classroom relationships between students and professors as a part of the liberal arts educational experience.

The lights slowly faded up as the video came to an end. A young white lady walked up to the lectern that suddenly appeared seemingly out of nowhere. She wore a navy blue sport coat . She looked so official. "Welcome to the University of Virginia. My name is Tina Landis. I graduated from the University of Virginia in 2013 and now work to recruit the best and the brightest to attend UVA in the admissions office. " She paused briefly before continuing. "When Thomas Jefferson built UVA, he had a vision for all of us, including the students to emerge as citizen scholars who are committed to improving the society in which we live. I stayed on to work here because UVA is home because it's where I found the people I want to be around, who I am impressed by, and inspired by daily. You will have peers who are pushing you to the next level, faculty who are trying to teach you new things. You have people who believe in you." She spoke with such passion. "Everyone here really wants to see you succeed, and it's that kind of environment that's just made me who I am today. I can honestly say that when I look back on my time here, these were some of the best years of my life."

She could be a walking commercial for UVA. That was convincing. She talked for another fifteen or twenty minutes about in-state tuition costs and housing and financial aid. She showed some slides with stats and other facts and figures. I will admit, though, I was stuck of the fact that there's no niggas on this campus.

Tina introduced some student ambassadors who would

show everyone around campus. "Let me introduce Kaleigh Watson, class of 2018, Dan Xia and Jacqueline Hoege, both freshman this year, and Zach Schauffler who is a senior this year. These students are committed and passionate about their UVA experience. You can ask them anything as you walk around the campus. If there's something they can't answer, just ask me when you're done with your tour. Because the group is so large, we're going to break you guys into groups, so the individual groups are not too large for our student ambassadors. So, if your first names start with A-D, you're going with Kaleigh, E-G, with Dan, H-M with Zac, and N-Z with Jacqueline. Ask them anything. They'll be honest with you. Yeah, right. Where the niggas at?

I introduced myself to Jacqueline. "Hi, I'm Nahim Lightbourne." She appeared friendly and not terribly scared of me. She didn't clutch her pearls or anything. We waited for any others to join our merry tribe before launching out. She marched us through Newcomb Hall. Once outside, we walked underneath a brick portico leading to a wide open lawn. Jacqueline began, "Discussion. Collaboration. Enlightenment. These are the ideals to which Thomas Jefferson aspired when conceiving the University of Virginia. In his quest to reinvent higher education in America, Jefferson sought to cultivate an environment in which students and faculty could live and learn from one another. At the University of Virginia, scholars and professors could exercise their ingenuity, develop the tools of self-governance and push the boundaries of knowledge in service to the common good. The result was a revolution: the Academical Village. This area was designed to foster cross-disciplinary exchange. Jefferson's design housed faculty from a range of specialties around a central Lawn. Students lived in single rooms between professors' homes. At the head of their shared Lawn stood the library (also known as the Rotunda). And at the Lawn's foot lay a panoramic view of the mountains, suggestive of the intellectual frontiers that lay open to discovery. Indeed, Jefferson's Academical Village gave physical shape to his ideals--ideals that would alter the course of higher education in America and the world." Jacqueline kept walking and talking. I would have been content standing right there taking in the sights of the grassy knoll. This is a beautiful campus!

Jacqueline began to ask people what their intended majors were. "Nahim?"

"Criminal Justice, but I am not absolutely sure yet."
The tour continued as did Jacqueline. "UVA is regarded as one of the most beautiful and prestigious universities in the world. In 1987, UNESCO named the University (in conjunction with Monticello) a World Heritage Site. This rare distinction has been bestowed upon only the world's most culturally significant landmarks. As a proud recipient of this honor, UVA sits alongside such renowned global sites as the Acropolis, the Galapagos Islands and the Pyramids of Giza. The University is one of only two such sites still being used for its original purpose."

We ambled down this tree-lined pathway. Jacqueline spun around on her heels. She entered "Since 1824, the University's gardens have served as a haven for study, conversation and reflection." Several ohs and ahhs echoed around the crowd.

As we toured the campus, Jacqueline was sure to point out the various academic buildings where our intended majors lived. "Sadly, Nahim, UVA does not have a major in criminal justice.

"That's okay. I told you I'm not sure yet that that's what I want to major in. It's just an area of interest now."

Chapter 17

Mrs. Mastrangelo waited patiently at the appointed location. I could see her from the distance as Jacqueline's team and I approached Newcomb Hall. She stood leaning alongside of the bus, her arms folded in apparent boredom. "What'd you think?" I heard her query from afar as she asked another student about their experiences on the tour. I yawned widely mouth agape accompanied by a massive sigh indicating how tired I was. It had been a long day since we had arrived in Charlottesville.

"Here's how the evening is going to go. We're going to load up the bus here and then go down the street to Maya restaurant. I've read good things about the food and the Yelp reviews are outstanding. We'll have dinner, and then we'll head to the hotel and get some sleep. How's that sound?"

"Mrs. M?" Riley wondered, "What kind of food does this Maya place serve?"

"The kind you eat." Mastrangelo answered with the precision of a wearied mother of multiple, whiny children who'd asked to many questions about dinner.

Once the bus loaded and we departed UVA, I opened my Yelp app and began to read aloud the reviews for my peers: "Had a really good dinner at Maya. I ordered the trout with a side of cheesy grits and leafy greens. The trout was cooked perfectly with a a nice crisp skin and moist inside. I was surprised how well the cooks de-boned the fish and how thick it was. It tasted excellent and was well seasoned. Would love to go back for more. The cheesy grits and leafy greens were a great side selection and both were very good. The only issue was the service which was good, but not great. I can't place my finger on it, the waiter was friendly enough but just seemed off on what he was doing.."

"Sounds good."

"Check this one out, guys." I read aloud. "We started with the mushroom plate which featured some local, organic mushrooms from Sharondale, plus a mini quiche, some asparagus, and a nice slice of pork belly."

"Yuck, I don't like mushrooms." A slight, feminine voice rang out.

"Then don't order mushrooms." Mastrangelo's comment snapped. I continued reading. "A tasty little sampler plate to get the palate buzzing. We also got the crispy cornmeal-crusted fried oysters which were plump, briny and perfectly crispy on the out-side--yum! Would definitely do those again." The students began buzzing about the review. People seemed rather excited about Maya. Hushing them to read another, I tried again. "Hold on, guys, listen to this one. 'I got their Sunday fried chicken special of the day with local beets and sweet potato fries as my sides, and my dining partner opted for the hanger steak, which isn't some-thing I'd usually order, but it came out looking beautifully, and we swapped half of each other's entrees so we could each enjoy both. Chicken was flavorful, juicy, with crispy-crunchy breading and a spicy lil pickle sauce for dipping. It was a healthy portion, especially with the pile of fries they stacked on my plate--mmmm, I ate it all. And the steak was so tender, really well seasoned and the red wine sauce was sweet and savory at the same time, it defi-nitely got me thinking twice about ignoring the steak next time I'm out at a restaurant as such."

"There's one more," I announced, "Jake, this one's aright up your alley—dessert. 'We ended the meal with a bang: their house made peanut butter fluff pie. Stacked high in layers of gra-ham cracker crust, chocolate, peanut butter, and whipped cream. Indulgent and a perfect American dessert.

Patty cooed. "I think this is going to be alright. I'm hun-gry."

The hostess dressed in black pants and a white blouse smiled at us and showed the lot to our table in the center of the room. "Mark and Lindsey will be your servers tonight. They'll be over soon to get your drink orders. Welcome to Maya. Enjoy." She bounced away on the balls of her feet. I'm ashamed (a little) for watching her booty as she went back to her station. Cute butt.

Mark and Lindsey appeared out of nowhere blocking my eyeline. "Hi, guys, welcome to Maya. I'm Mark. This is Lindsey.

We're going to be taking care of you tonight. I will be taking orders from this side of the table." Gesturing with his right hand, "And Linz will take the other side. Let's start right here." They went down their respective sides. Most of the students ordered Pepsi and root beer. When Lindsey sidled up to me and asked what I wanted, I ordered sweet tea. Actually, I ordered an Arnold Palmer because I figured a southern restaurant would have real lemonade—not that premade Kool-aid stuff.

Mrs. Mastrangelo gathered everyone's attention to her. "So, guys, I'd love to hear your reaction to visiting UVA today. What'd you think? Doug, what about you get us started?"

"It was alright. Nothing fantastic. Beautiful campus, but the dorms were old fashioned and stuffy."

"Yes, they were" shot in Marion.

Several others shared their opinions of the campus visit. I really hadn't planned to register my misgivings, but..."

"Nahim, what did you think?"

"Hmm...what else can I say? That campus is beautiful. Did you guys see those rooms on 'The Lawn'?"

That lit up the table. "OMG, so cute! Anna cooed." My tour guide said "Each room is furnished with a lofted bed with ladder above a daybed with cover, a secretary desk with chair, a hutch containing a refrigerator with freezer and a microwave, a built-in closet and sink closet, and a rocking chair."

"And most of the rooms have fireplaces, I praised. "The only downside about them, though, it's all fourth year housing. I'll have to wait three years to be able to apply to maybe get in. No air conditioning either. I can imagine chilling outside on the deck when a nice breeze blows through. Plus, they're singles—no roommates."

"That's the best part of it. Not having to smell anybody else's funk."

"Or farts."

"Thank you, Trevor. Nice dinner table talk." Mrs. Mastrangelo—ever the mom.

Soon, Mark and Lindsey interrupted our conversation to take everyone's meal orders.

"I know what Nahim wants. Fried chicken, greens, and

black eyed peas. 'Him look! They've got watermelon granita for dessert."

Not gonna lie, I gristled at the comment, but it was the quiet laughs that dug at me more. No one spoke out against this blatant racist attack. I hate these people. I can't go off though. We are hundreds of miles from home. I wish I could call Dr. Davis for advice. He'd know what to do.

"You know what, Wesley? I think I will have the chicken. I thought I wanted the crab cakes, but you can't go wrong with down home fried chicken." I smugly turned towards Mark to share my order.

The evening's meal dragged on as I refused to speak to anyone the rest of dinner. Not wishing to be rude, I only spoke to Mark or Lindsey the rest of the night. Yelp did not lie, that peanut butter pie was ridiculous! So good.

We finished up our meals and boarded the bus to go to Courtyard by Marriot for the evening.

"You are paired with your buddy from this morning in the hotel. That's going to be your roommate for the night. Please stay in you rooms. No roaming the hotel or going outside. I can trust you all, right?"

"Yes, Mrs. Mastrangelo." The chorus of singsong affirmations sounded much like a cacophony of third graders. She dutifully called the partners' names to present their room keys. She called my name and I skulked to the bottom of the bus to grab my stowed luggage and then up the elevator and to my room. I didn't want to talk to anyone—not even the roommate.

I grabbed my laptop and swaddled beneath the blankets for my solo hibernation. First web search "University of Virginia." I searched the site for clues to the no-black-people mystery. I searched for a Black Student Union. The link led to the Multicultural Student Center.

"Ooh, second floor of Newcomb Hall. I remember where that is." I settled in my mind to visit the Center the next day when we go back to campus.

Once we were loaded onto the bus, Mrs. Mastrangelo laid out the game plan for the day. We would have about five hours to explore the campus on our own and would meet up for a later lunch before hitting the road.

I took my leave and separated from the group making a beeline for Newcomb Hall. Walking purposely up the large set of white stairs, I passed the mail room and a couple of eateries. This place is cool. At the top of the stairs, there were no signs instructing where to go, so I turned to the left. After a few steps, my destination appeared before me. A couple Asian females exited the glass doors. They smiled ss they chatted about their next adventures. Like a gentleman, I waited for them to fully exit (I held the door) and then made my entrance. Couches lined the space. A full library of books decorated the walls.. I slowly and quietly peeked around the room. There were small conference rooms and offices—each room decorated with ethnic garb and kitsch defining the space's ownership. I noted the door covered with kente cloth and a poster of Malcolm X, Martin Luther King, and President Obama. I expected to find my Nubian treasure. I was right.

I stopped just outside the door and peeked in—hoping not to be bothering or interrupting—there appeared a large-sized black male seated behind the desk. The K-A-Psi Greek letters leaped from his red-and-white sweatshirt.

"Excuse me. I'm looking for the Black Student Union."

"You've found it." He had just taken a huge bite from a sandwich. He stood while wiping his hands and mouth with a brown paper napkin. He extended his hand for me to shake. "Leroy Johnson, president of the Black Student Alliance. The booming tenor of his voiced equaled the size of his massive physique." "What can I do to help you?"

"My name is Nahim Lightbourne, and I'm here visiting UVA with my high school. We've been here for a couple days, and I'm a little concerned."

"Concerned? That's odd. What's on your mind?"

"I've been wondering..." Not sure I am really wanting to ask, I looked around, quieted my voice. I looked over my shoulder as if I had some great secret to tell, "Where all the niggas at?"

Leroy burst out a robust laugh. "Man, there's a whole bunch of us here. Where you been looking? We have a big cookout thing every Friday. 'Black Friday' is what we call it. Wall to wall brothas and sistas. Spades, pitty pat, dominoes everywhere. Dining services provides ribs, greens, and macaroni & cheese."

"Whew! I'm glad to hear you say that. We came for an admissions tour yesterday, and I noted there weren't many of us in the admissions video.

"I was in that video. Matter of fact, I was wearing this exact sweatshirt."

Embarrassed at my own ignorance, I sheeped, "Oh, I'm sorry."

"A common thought. I mean, we're no HBCU, but there are quite a few of us here. A number of them hang out here—well, not right now, obviously, but after classes. Anything else I can answer for you?"

"This school was founded by Thomas Jefferson, right? I know he was a president and all, but wasn't he also a slave owner? Everyone is celebrating his time in the White House, but I haven't heard anyone mention the latter. It's hard for me to imagine coming to school here and the truth is being whitewashed and sugarcoated."

"Oh, I feel ya, good brotha. I felt the same way until I took Professor Grimes' class and we went to Montpelier."

"Montpelier? Was that Jefferson's plantation?

"It's not too far from here, actually. Maybe about 45 minutes." Leroy looked at his watch. "Yeah, she might be over there." "You got a couple minutes? I want you to meet her. She usually has office hours right now. She could probably give you a better answer than me, no doubt."

"Sure. I've got some time."

Leroy packed up his belongings and grabbed his keys on the blue lanyard from in front of the computer. I stood up and he directed me to exit the office. He closed the door behind us. He spoke to the person behind the main desk whom I didn't see before. He told her where we were going and that he'd be back in a little bit.

We stepped outside and were hit with a cloud of heat and humidity. "Good Lord, it's hotter than blue blazes out here! It was freezing when I left my apartment this morning. I guess I don't need this sweatshirt anymore." He unsheathed himself of the fleece cocoon.

"Alright. Let's go see her. She's over in the Curry School.

Chapter 18

"Dr. Grimes, I am really struggling with the idea that this college was founded by Thomas Jefferson. He owned slaves. Hell, pardon my French, it was probably built by slaves. It's hard to imagine living or learning here."

"Young man, the stench of slavery is all over America. We can't hide from it. We've got to embrace history if we're going to learn from it."

"I get what you're saying, but it's hard!"

"No doubt." She smoothed her short, natural cut. Her waves were popping. "The American educational system has not prepared you well for getting over colonialism. White folks would rather imagine that slavery never happened. Black folks too." She paused. "I teach social studies. In fact, I teach students who want to be social studies teachers—most of whom are white. If they're going to do it well, they have to be confronted by real history. That's why every semester, the Curry School sponsors a field trip where I take students to Montpelier."

Looking confused, Nahim asked, "What's Montpelier? I feel like I've heard of that before."

"Here in Charlottesville, we are but a 45-minute drive to Montpelier, home of Founding Father James Madison, America's fourth president. There students learn about the life of Paul Jennings – a man born into slavery at Montpelier who would eventually publish his own memoir. On our last visit, they listened to the voice of Rebecca Gilmore-Coleman, a descendant of the enslaved community at Montpelier, discuss the legacies of slavery in contemporary society. They discussed how James Madison, who helped enshrine freedom in the American constitution, never freed a slave."

Feeling righteously indignant, Nahim declared, "See, that's what I'm talking about. America lies about freedom and justice and equality. That's a load of bull."

"And this is why I persist. Through real, human stories, past and present, it's important that students learn about the history that is recorded and the history that is lost – and, perhaps most important, the history that is still being uncovered."

"So, wait. Montpelier is a former plantation. How can you take students there? Field trips are supposed to be fun. A plantation sounds horrible."

Grimes had an answer for every one of Nahim's concerns. She spoke of the value of place-based learning, what she called "learning through experience."

"I can't believe you get away with that. Those places need to be burned to the ground."

"I was right where you are thirty years ago, but I've evolved some in my thinking. There is just something about being in the actual spaces. The stories become more salient when you can experience how small the rooms were, or how far families had to walk to see each other. You can't get that from a book. You can't get it from a podcast. I always ask students for their feedback and evaluation. One student said '"I think it's important to go past that – to dig a little deeper,' She said 'Definitely what I learned today will help me in the future to dig deeper for my students.'"" Grimes continued, "As a teacher, researcher and educator, I have always believed in field experiences and place-based experiences. Getting outside the classroom and helping students learn to act in their immediate community and world has always been a fundamental premise of how I want to teach. By modeling experiential learning for future teachers, the Montpelier experience is an ideal case study," Grimes said.

"But how does this help the black students here at UVA?" Nahim returned to the reason why Leroy wanted him to talk to this lady.

"It's all a part of my grand scheme. My research helps the entire Curry School to support teachers everywhere with research-based approaches to increase racial, religious and ethnic inclusion. If my research is effective, it can have much farther reaches than just UVA. Like it or not, the story of slavery is built into our American DNA," Grimes said. "The Constitution that we talk about was a product of men who were slaveholders. There's a duality to this historical narrative that it's important that we tell. It's important because it's the truth, and it's important because everyone has a part in this American story.

"I just really need to think about this stuff. What you're saying makes a whole lotta sense...intellectually... but something just ain't right about y'all seeming to celebrate slavery."

"What I ask students and myself is 'How do we make all of this information useful, accessible and actionable? And how do we contextualize it today? By continually asking these questions, and working to tell the individual human stories behind every artifact, the goal is to bring the multi-layered identity of the enslaved to life, to make them human."

"My American Studies teacher, Dr. Davis, would just love you!

"Leroy, don't let me hog all the conversation. What's it really like for the black students here?"

"I already told you about Black Fridays. Free food and everything. It's a time when all the black folks on campus get together and eat. It's like a family reunion. A real safe space where we don't have to front with white folks around. The music is loud and when that beat drops, Mannn! You can dance to it and not worry about what you're doing."

"That sounds dope," Nahim grinned while rubbing his hands together.

"Tell him about 'black bus stop.'"

"Oh yeah, the "black bus stop," has been historically a hangout place for black students, though it's not used really the way it used to be by the black student population. ... It used to be much bigger. My understanding is that sometimes black alums from the 70s and 80s come through and drop science on the current students." Leroy paused in reflection and his excited tone calmed, "I don't want to make it seem like it's Mecca here all the time. Sometimes, it's a real challenge to be black at UVA. I go to the Bus Stop and Black Fridays to fill my tank, so I can deal with these people. I left there singing, 'I'm black y'all. I'm black y'all. I'm bliggity, bliggity, black y'all!'" Dr. Grimes mimicked Leroy's hip hop style moves.

The entire bus ride home Nahim kept quoting Leroy's song, "I'm black y'all. I'm black y'all. I'm bliggity, bliggity, black y'all!"

"Oh, shut up, Nahim! We get it. You're black."

Once we were loaded onto the bus, Mrs. Mastrangelo laid out the game plan for the day. We would have about five hours to explore the campus on our own and would meet up for a later lunch before hitting the road.

I took my leave and separated from the group making a beeline for Newcomb Hall. Walking purposely up the large set of white stairs, I passed the mail room and a couple of eateries. This place is cool. At the top of the stairs, there were no signs instructing where to go, so I turned to the left. After a few steps, my destination appeared before me. A couple Asian females exited the glass doors. They smiled ss they chatted about their next adventures. Like a gentleman, I waited for them to fully exit (I held the door) and then made my entrance. Couches lined the space. A full library of books decorated the walls.. I slowly and quietly peeked around the room. There were small conference rooms and offices—each room decorated with ethnic garb and kitsch defining the space's ownership. I noted the door covered with kente cloth and a poster of Malcolm X, Martin Luther King, and President Obama. I expected to find my Nubian treasure. I was right.

I stopped just outside the door and peeked in—hoping not to be bothering or interrupting—there appeared a large-sized black male seated behind the desk. The K-A-Psi Greek letters leaped from his red-and-white sweatshirt.

"Excuse me. I'm looking for the Black Student Union."

"You've found it." He had just taken a huge bite from a sandwich. He stood while wiping his hands and mouth with a brown paper napkin. He extended his hand for me to shake. "Leroy Johnson, president of the Black Student Alliance. The booming tenor of his voiced equaled the size of his massive physique."

"What can I do to help you?"

"My name is Nahim Lightbourne, and I'm here visiting UVA with my high school. We've been here for a couple days, and I'm a little concerned."

"Concerned? That's odd. What's on your mind?"

Chapter 19

"I love you, babe. I'm so glad you're back."

"Me too." Nahim cooed as he embraced Jolene's frame. He leaned in for a kiss. His lips met Jolene's. Their lip lock turned into a full-on petting session. Before Jolene had realized it, Nahim had slid himself and Jolene behind a bush near the front of the school. Jolene had been so caught up, she was unaware. Their kissing was passionate. Nahim's full lips engulfed her thin lips, especially when his tongue explored her mouth.

As they kissed, Jolene took notice of Nahim's hands as they slid down her back and landed on her backside. She liked the feeling, especially as the warmth from his inner temperature began to heat up. She began to enjoy it too much. Realizing this, she took a step backward. "Nahim, the rules." She opened her elbows outward to break his connection. The two took a pause from their embrace. Breathy and slightly intoxicated, Jolene added "Boy, I love kissing you. Your lips are so soft. I get lost in your kisses. I lose all sense of everything else."

"I hear ya." Nahim asserted. "I could love living here. Wanna come over tonight and watch a movie? I heard about this movie on Netflix called 'The Fault in Our Stars.' I have heard good things. It's about these kids who have cancer and start dating. We could watch Netflix and chill out."

"Nahim, I know what that phrase means. I'm saved not stupid." Nahim thought Jolene's attempt to look stern especially cute.

"Seriously, I just want to chill out. Every part of my life is so scheduled. I rarely get time to just kick back. I just want some time with my favorite girl; I just want to watch 'The Fault in Our Stars' next to my girl."

"Ok. I'd like that. That sounds interesting. Your mom will be there, I imagine? The young lady bounced away as she left her paramour. She was almost giddy. "I've got to get going to get to the church for youth group."

"Babe, why you worrying? The church is a block away from the school. Why don't we meet up out front afterwards and then we can catch the bus to my house?"

"Ok. I will let my dad know not to expect me until late." Nahim watched her as she went down the sidewalk. His eyes hungered as he watched her wander off. Damn! That girl is foin! Nahim watched for as long as he could visibly see her sweet frame. Ninety minutes later, Nahim emerged from the double doors of the gymnasium. Jolene sat on the pedestal at the bottom of the steps on the front of the school. Nahim's smile widened as he approached. When he got close enough, he gingerly leaned in and kissed her neck. "Hey cutie. You been waiting' long?"

"Not long, but I would wait for you forever." Jolene feigned a Southern belle as she fanned herself with her hand. "You, sir, are worth waiting for." After a long pause, Jolene blurted, "You are going to have to introduce yourself to my dad someday soon."

Nahim was sipping from his water bottle at the same time Jolene mentioned her dad. He choked and spit out some of the liquid. "What? Why? When?" he gasped. "Well, when I told my dad I would be going to your house, I told him your mom was going to be there to supervise us. I think he felt some kinda way about me meeting your mom before he had the chance to meet you." He is a little old fashioned."

Sputtering over his words, "Are we there yet? The meeting of parents thing?"

"I guess so. You said your mom was going to be there. Dad said I can't go if there is no parental supervision. She is going to be home, right? I hope I did not just lie to my dad."
Sweating as he had not yet informed his mom they were having company. His eyes averted, "No, you did not lie. She will be there. And my little brothers too."

"Ok. Let's go. I don't want to be out too too late." She thought of the lengthy bus ride she would have to endure.

On the long journey, Jolene and Nahim snuggled in the seat in the rear of the bus. They silently giggled as they "people watched." The Asian businessman, for instance, who decided to stand instead of sitting. He fell asleep standing up holding onto one of the hand straps. His head was cranked back, a slight snore emanating from his open mouth. It must have been a long day for several of the commuters.

"Look, look! She is sleep for real!" Nahim pointed at a middle-aged black woman leaning forward as she slept—her mouth wide open with her nose pressed against the silver bar atop the seat back in front of her. "She looks like a pig."

"Nahim! That's rude!" She slapped his arm.

"I'm not trying to be rude. Look at her. Her hair is all slicked backward and her nose looks like a snout all pressed up against that bar. Plus, she has the nerve to be wearing all pink. You can't tell me she doesn't look like a pig." The woman's black skin really stood out against her big golden hoop earrings and her pink shirt. "She looks like she planned to fall asleep. She even put her glasses on top of her head. Just then, the sleeping woman released an oinkish snort snore.

"Ooh, honey! Maybe you are right." Jolene giggled.

"And would you look at that guy over there? Adolph Hitler is riding on our bus." Nahim spoke of the white man with a horrible black toupee with his cropped mustache. The man had wrapped himself in a red tartan-plaid blanket. The couple giggled at the fact that the Fuhrer had to take the Number 17 city bus. "Watch this." When Hitler reached his stop, he picked up his belongings and disembarked. As soon as his feet touched the pavement, Nahim yelled out, "Heil, Hitler and mimicked the Nazi salute with his right arm outstretched. The gentlemen apparently heard the quip, and spun on his heels. He yelled, "Fich dich, Schwarz!" His middle finger extended. Jolene about rolled onto the floor and erupted in laughter.

"I wonder what he said."

"He probably said F-you, nigger!."

The young couple continued laughing for an extended period. After a brief time, Jolene leaned onto Nahim's chest and shoulders. Pretty soon, she was fast asleep.

"JoJo, wake up. We are almost at our stop." Nahim got a kick out of the fact that Jolene purred while she slept. He was glad she felt comfortable enough to come to the 'hood. She did not even flinch when they practically had to step over a homeless man after alighting the steps of the bus.

"Excuse me, sir" Jolene whispered as she stretched over his pile."

"Look at you—all proper."

"I know you are making fun of me, but just because he is homeless doesn't mean he is not a human being worthy of respect and dignity."

Nahim sloughed, "Ah, he is a bum. What has he done to earn my respect?"

"Nahim, I can't believe you. What would Sister Maya say?" Mimicking Dr. Angelou "That man is a child of God. You're a child of God and I am a child of God, and one of the difficult things for me is to realize and keep in front of my understanding is that the brute, the bigot, and the batterer is also a child of God--whether he knows it or not; you are supposed to know it and treat him accordingly!"

"You are lucky you are so cute. I might've had to bust you in your lip for doing a black voice." He had to admit the cadence and voice pattern were a dead-on match for Maya Angelou's.

Chapter 20

"Baby, I got in!" Nahim practically rammed his acceptance letter from UVA in Jolene's face.

Holding his hand at bay, "I didn't even realize you had applied. Congratulations...I guess."

"What do you mean 'you guess.' You're not excited for me? I got into my first choice school."

"Excited? I didn't even know about it. How am I supposed to be excited? If anything, I'm furious."

"Furious? With me? Why?"

"Because you don't respect me," she huffed. "You don't respect this relationship."

"How can you say that? I love you," he pleaded.

Jolene's face turned serious. "Nahim, UVA is 15 hours away from me. You know long-distance relationships don't work!"
"Babe, we're strong enough to hack it. In fact, in just two short years, you can join me there."

"I can't leave my dad alone like that. I'll just go somewhere close. Ooh, what if you went to Tulane, Xavier, or maybe even LSU?"

"Is there any reason all the schools you suggested are all HBCUs?" Nahim smiled to alert Jolene he was joking.

"What's wrong with a historically black college? It's something to consider."

Pressing his point, "But UVA is offering a full ride scholarship. I sincerely doubt an HBCU can do that. Besides, I already visited those schools. Aside from the history, I wasn't impressed. I mean, UVA had a Popeye's/Cold Stone combo!"

"Nahim, no one is that stupid to base their college decision on a fast food restaurant!"

"Dr. Davis told me he chose his college because he had heard there was a Wendy's on campus."

"If that's true, it's ridiculous! But, I sincerely doubt that was his rationale."

Confident and sure Nahim asserted, "It's true. He told me he felt so fooled when he showed up and learned the nearest Wendy's was a forty-minute drive away. Besides, it wasn't because he just likes Frosty's that much. He said he was working at a Wendy's at the time, and he knew he would need to be paying for college himself, so he figured he could get a job transfer."

"Well, that makes more sense." Turning the conversation, "What did your mom say?"

"That's a WHOLE 'NOTHA STORY! When I shared the news with her, she was baking sweet potato pies. Every other word, she muttered 'My baby is leaving me.' She cried all in the batter. Those were some salty pies." Nahim paused, "Even though she was sad, I think she was still excited though. She loves me," he mocked. "I don't think I'm black enough to go to an HBCU."

"What? Now you're really not making sense."

"Think about it. I've been attending this lily-white school for the past four years. I've just started reading Malcolm X, for goodness' sake. I don't even own a pair of Tims. My mom makes me wear my pants above my navel. I probably wouldn't fit in."

"But you'll fit in at UVA?"

"Here, there, I'm special. The magic Negro. I'm a different breed in white spaces. I don't know if I have what it takes to stand out among other black folks. At Hilton, I run circles around those white boys." Nahim paused. "You know, I do need to go visit Dillard. I follow the president on Twitter. He goes by the name @ hiphopprez. I really like his posts. He always posts about inviting students to his house for meals. Occasionally, he posts pictures of the campus. It looks beautiful there. I need to talk to Dr. D for some advice."

"It doesn't matter where you apply. With your grades, anywhere you apply, you'll get in."

"It's not that I worry about not getting in. I'm looking for someplace to call home for four years or more. Doc told me when I find it, I'll know. When I left UVA, I just felt like that my place was there. Like there was a future there for me. Like I'm taking a step towards growing up into something."

"Babe," Jolene stepped forward and held Nahim's face on her hands, "I'm very excited for you. I just don't know what I'm gonna do without you near me every day. I'm just scared you'll go off to Charlottesville, find someone new, and forget all about me." Pushing her away playfully, "JoJo, I love you, that's impossible. We'll have FaceTime, Skype, email, Insta. Plus, I'll be home for breaks and stuff. You're not getting rid of me that easily. We can do this."

Chapter 21

"Ms. Lightbourne, thank you so much for letting me crash your holiday dinner. It smells so good in here. Since my dad is away at a conference, I thought I would be alone having PB&J." "Honey, don't you mention it. We have enough to feed an army." She was right. The bounty spread across the center of the table and the two counters circling the kitchen. The table in the dining room was set formally.

"Now that everybody is here, let's get ready to eat. Circle up." Ms. Lightbourne's instruction set the formation into action. The family members each marched into place around the kitchen table. "Jolene, typically, saying the grace is the responsibility of the oldest person in the room, but as that falls to me this year, I am wondering if you would do the honor?"

"Oh," Jolene stumbled, "yes ma'am. I'd be happy to." Ms. Lightbourne instructed everyone to bow their heads.

Jolene wanted to make a good impression. She prayed, "Gracious Heavenly Father, we gather today surrounded by family and friends, we are grateful for your blessings and your goodness. Bless this house, this family, and its matriarch," Jolene opened her eyes and saw the smiling nod of Nahim's mother; she knew her prayer was working, "bless the food we're about to receive and the hands that prepared it. In Jesus' name we pray."

Nahim thought the prayer had ended, but Jolene continued, "Could you all repeat after me? We make no excuse for the things we have here for the things we have here God has provided and for this we are grateful, Amen." A chorus of "Amens" followed. At that, the next sounds were plates and silverware. Jolene appreciated this responsive recitation she had learned at church.

"Ooh, babe. Come take a selfie with me by the turkey. This food looks like it could be in a magazine." Nahim gave a cheesy grin as Jolene extended her right arm above them. Her phone poised to capture the moment. Jolene posed her duck lips next to

Nahim's cheek.

"Baby, sit down, I'll fix your plate. It gets kinda crazy at this time. What do you want?" Jolene felt an honored guest as Nahim fawned over her."

"A little bit of everything, please."

"Are you sure? There's a lot of food in there."

"Nahim, your mom went through a lot of trouble to make this feast, so I'm going to eat it. Plus, my dad always says the Christian thing to do is to eat what is set before you."

"O-K." He rolled his eyes; Nahim knew she'd be literally biting off more than she could chew. He kept his eyes on her as she ate her meal--wondering when she'd tap out, but she kept plowing. Every so often, she'd pause to ask "What is this?" when she'd come across something unfamiliar. "What are these weeds?"

"Those are greens."

"I use a mix of turnips and mustard greens," Mom Lightbourne interjected. They're a little spicy, but you can tame that by adding a teaspoon of apple cider vinegar to take the bite away."

"And what are these grey, wrinkly things?"

"Oh, those are chitlins. You don't want to know. But taste them, you might like them."

Jolene stirred the chitlins with her fork before cautiously taking a mouthful. "Interesting, a little chewy. That's an odd flavor." She kept chewing. Leaning over, she whispered, "Nahim, what's a chitlin?"

"Chitlins are pig intestines. The full name is chitterlings." Jolene greened as she realized she had just ingested the intestines of an animal.

"Intestines? Why would ANYONE willingly eat pig intestines?"

Mom added, "Back in slavery days, food was limited. The masters' family got the best parts of the pig and they gave the slaves what was left over. My ancestors learned to make the most out of the worst. They'd clean the dookie literally scraping the membrane and boiling the shit out of them. That's what's at the heart of soul food cooking. What your ancestors thought was a punishment just taught us how to survive." It was that survival instinct that kept our people through 200 years of brutal oppression.

"I'm sorry." Jolene lowered her eyes and head.

"No, honey. Nothing to apologize about. In this house, we celebrate and honor the strength of the slave. They were over-comers. Slavery should have took them out, but with the help of God, we're still here."

Jolene managed a smile, but, she still ate the rest of her meal without saying much else. When she finished, she went back into the kitchen to get dessert. The counter was full of several different pies, a coconut pound cake, and a casserole pan covered with Nilla wafers. She could tell there was something custardy under the cookies. She lifted one of the cookies with the spatula when Nahim chimed in, "That's banana pudding." Nahim's deep baritone coming from over her shoulder assuaged her confusion. "Is that pumpkin pie? I love pumpkin pie." Jolene pointed at the orange-ish brown circle on the counter.

"Hell no, that ain't no pumpkin pie. That's a sweet pota-to pie. This is a black house!" Again, Jolene felt ashamed at Ms. Lightbourne's chastisement.

Jolene sat down with her dessert; she chose to get what Nahim described as "the hookup" (a faux cheesecake with cherries slathered across the top). She scooped a spoonful into her mouth. "Mmm...Ms. Lightbourne, this is heavenly!"

"Oh, thank you, baby. You want some coffee?"

"Oh, yes ma'am. Thank you."

"How do you like it?"

"Like I like my man, black and sweet." Jolene thought herself clever as evidenced by her winsome grin and wink towards Nahim.

"Hmph." Mom Lightbourne tooted her lips in derision.

After a few moments enjoying dessert, almost like clock-work, with no coordination or instruction, people began to align themselves in formation to clean up. Within what seemed like moments--dishes washed and dried. Where piles of food once set, cleaned dishes stacked. For chores, this time seemed as much as the fellowship over dinner. There was singing and dancing; R. Kelly's "Step in the Name of Love" got the crowd riled. Somehow Jolene found herself gyrating down a Soul Train line. Someone started a bubble fight with the suds from the dishwater.

The flurry of activity slowed and people began to curl up on the living room sofas. Nahim's Aunt Yolanda put a Tyler Perry Madea play in the DVD player. By the end of the second song, the sounds of snoring enveloped the room.

"Come on," Nahim pulled at Jolene's arm, "Let's go to my room."

Jolene followed his direction down the hallway. Nahim ushered her into the room. A large Lebron James poster greeted those who entered.

"I can't stand Madea plays. Every other word is a song where someone is screaming at you. Let's watch something else. He closed the door quietly and turned out the lights. He picked up the black remote control using it to press play on the player and turned to activate the TV .

Jolene grabbed a pillow as she sat down on the bed. "What are we watching?"

The Netflix app logo flashed across the screen. Nahim searched in the streaming menu. "Tyler told me to watch this. It's called Blue is the Warmest Color. It's a love story."

" Oh, that's good. You and me and a good love story." The action of the film started without any opening credits. The camera focused on a white girl who emerged from her house and got on a school bus. There was no sound or dialogue for a full two minutes. In fact, the unnamed girl got on the bus and went to sleep. When dialogue began, it was in French.

"Ugh, it's a foreign film? I don't want to read a whole movie." Jolene's nose crinkled in anger... or was it disgust? Whatever it was, Nahim did not find it cute.

"Just give it a chance. It can't be all bad or Ty wouldn't have recommended it, right? Let's just keep watching."

For the greater part of fifteen minutes, the camera followed the white girl as she went to several classes including her literature class. Nahim questioned how it could be a love story without the presence of a leading man. Soon, Adele, the white girl, is having lunch with Thomas as they discuss a book from class. Jolene disquieted when Thomas mentioned the book's character as he describes how the Marquis "says he loves her, but he's writing on a whore's back."

"Uhm. I hope this movie is not full of bad language like that."

Nahim laughed as Jolene showed her more parochial and conservative style. "Keep watching..." he pandered.

Thomas continues to talk to Adele about *The Life of Marianne*, a 600-page novel, because Adele asked him to read it.

Thomas admits, "I'll read it. I don't give a fuck."

"Nahim!"

"Babe, I didn't know! I've never seen this movie before either. You don't have to hit me anymore." He rubbed his thigh where she slapped.

The scene changed to Adele and Thomas in a darkened movie theater. The camera showed Thomas looking down fondly.

"Was that his thing? Nahim!"

"I don't think so. They were just trying to hold hands. Relax." He cooed to try to calm her down.

Soon, Adele is getting undressed in her bedroom. She's asleep in her bed and a pair of hands begins to massage her and play sexually as Adele begins to undulate.

"Who's that guy with the blue hair? That's not Thomas. Oh, wait. That's a girl! Ewww, that's two girls getting it on, yuck! Adele is dreaming about having sex with a girl."

"It's not a big deal, babe. It's just a movie."

"Just a movie, huh? Romans 1:26 says 'For this cause God gave them up unto vile affections: for even their women did change the natural use into that which is against nature.'"

"Just watch the movie with me, will you please?" Nahim leaned over and kissed Jolene's neck and nuzzled in her ear. "That's probably the worst of it."

"OK. For you, I'll watch. I hope it doesn't get worse." Jolene nestled back into the couch along the wall.

A few scenes later, Thomas and Adele end up having sex. The camera focuses on Adele's bare butt and on her naked breasts. The two moan and thrust. Even though Adele sits atop Thomas' naked body, you don't see any parts of him.

"That's not a hand! Don't even try to tell me that was his hand. THAT is his thingy!" Jolene sat forward in her place and

gripped the pillow tightly. "It's so big! I have never seen one before. Is that what it looks like?"

"There are bigger ones than that." Nahim chuckled as he
thought of himself. "See, that girl was a fluke. It's not 'vile' or
'unnatural' as you say. Let's just keep watching.
The blossoming sexual relationship between the characters tit-
illated Nahim. Later in the film when the blue-haired boy was
replaced by Emma, the lesbianic sex turned graphic and Nahim,
semi-embarrassed by his semi-visible arousal, Nahim shifted his
jeans and covered his lap with a pillow. "Aww, man." All at once,
Nahim regretted his choice to wear skinny jeans today. He again
tried to readjust.

Leaning up from his chest, Jolene inquired, "Everything
alright?"

"Just trying to get comfortable."

Nahim pulled at his crotch area. Noticing the cause of his
consternation, Jolene cooed, "Need some help with that?"

"You sure?" Nahim spread himself on the couch while slid-
ing lower on the cushion. He opened his legs wide to give Jolene
space. She put her left hand on this right thigh and got a truer
sense of how tight his jeans really were. "How are you breathing
in these things?" Nahim chuckled.

Jolene wrestled as she tried to work the zipper of Nahim's
jeans with one hand. "Here. Let me help you," Nahim toyed. He
moved his hands to his crotch and slowly unzipped his trousers.
He even unbuttoned to give Jolene unfettered easier access. His
semi-erect manhood teased from the slit in his boxer shorts.

"Can I turn the lights back on? I wanna see this?" Jolene
surprised herself with her forwardness. She reset her position
next to Nahim. As she sat, she leaned in for a deep kiss. As the
passion flared, she allowed her hands to explore. When her hand
brushed his member, Jolene abruptly stopped, "Ooh, can I touch
it?" Nahim widened intimating his consent. Jolene playfully
ran her fingernail up Nahim's muscular inner thigh. She firmly
grasped his joystick when suddenly it jumped in her hand. Laughing, "What was that?"

He shrugged, "It has a mind of its own."

"Nu-uh. You did that. Can you make it happen again?"

"You've got to do the same thing you were doing before." Nahim winked as he repositioned wider. "Wait, do you wanna kiss it?"

"Him!"

Nahim thought Jolene's innocence alluring. The two played that way for a few more minutes. "When she made mention of Nahim's size, the stick stiffened nearly straight from within its cotton sheath. "Yeah, can I kiss it?" Jolene sweetly undertoned. Jolene leaned down and her lips parted to receive her prize. Just then the door swung open.

"Whatchall doing?" Nahim's younger brother smiled from the threshold. "Ooh, I'm gonna tell mom...Momma!" He quickly turned and ran down the hall towards the living room. Nahim wanted to chase, but he was in no condition.

"Oh, Jesus! Shit! Shit! Shit! I better go." The couple rushed to straighten themselves to hide their play. Jolene skedaddled out the door thanking Ms. Lightbourne for her hospitality. Nahim stood stunned as he had when he heard Jolene cuss for the first time.

She sped home in her father's borrowed car. As she drove, the shame and guilt overwhelmed. She regretted allowing herself to go so far. For letting her guard down so low. She cried out, "Jesus, I am so sorry. Please forgive me." She repeated that phrase multiple times as she traversed the city. When she arrived at home, she ran straight upstairs to her room. She removed her clothes and put on her nightgown. In the darkness, she let out a final scream while staring upwards, "God! Please forgive me. If you forgive me, I will never do it again." Afterwards she huffed then buried her face into the pillow and drifted off to sleep. A while later her phone buzzed. Without turning the lights on, Jolene bumbled until she could see the bright screen. The screen read, "U up?"

Jolene warmed and wiped the sleep from her eyes. She replied to the text that she was awake. The next buzz indicated "I'm downstairs. Let me in." Jolene couldn't believe it. Nahim had travelled all the way out to her house. She quickly ran to the bathroom and freshened her makeup and took a big swig of mouthwash and spat into the sink. Before she ran down the stairs, she took one last look into the mirror. Satisfied of her cuteness, Jolene tried to skip two steps at a time. She slipped on the carpeted stairs. Blushing, she straightened herself, turned on the front porch light, and stood face-to-face with her boyfriend. She coyed with a wink as she opened wide the front door.

"Nahim, what are you doing all the way out here?"

Nahim stepped inside and grabbed Jolene around the waist and drew her near for a sloppy, wet kiss. Hollywood style, he scooped her up in his strong arms and carried her up the steps like she weighed next to nothing. At the top of the stairs, he breathily asked, "Which way to your bedroom?"

"That way." Jolene pointed in the left direction. She kissed him deeply as he lay her on the mussed duvet. Nahim was able to make out the large butterfly with its wings spread wide.

"So girly. It's so cute!" She knew his sarcasm was meant to belittle her chastity.

The pre-dawn light pressing its way through the curtains disturbed Jolene's slumber enough to wrest her eyes open. In the haze of awake, she caught a brief glimpse of Nahim's muscular backside as he pulled his underwear up and pants on.

"What time is it?" she grogged.

"I tried not to wake you. It's 5:30 in the morning. I've got to get home before my mom wakes up. She usually has to be at work by 7:30. I'll have hell to pay if I'm not there when she gets moving around." By this time, Jolene had stirred herself awake and had sat up in the bed—the sheets no longer covering. "I don't want to go." As he spoke, he slowly approached the bed, Nahim purred as he reached for her loose boob. He pinched and cupped. Bending over, he kissed her perky nipple.

Parting his lips, Nahim suckled her mam. Jolene wooed at his attention. She ran her hands through his hair grabbing a handful and tugging lightly. "I better go. Let me go use the bathroom before I get on the long bus ride. I'll text you when I get home."

"Ok. Bye, baby. I love you."

"Love you too.

Jolene exhaled and satisfied-smiled as she lie backwards onto her mattress. She didn't even walk Nahim out. She put her hands behind her head on the pillow. Her bosoms separated as she reclined. "Ahh, I love him."

"Jolene. Jolene. I'm home." Rev. Young tried to arouse his daughter.

Jolene recoiled in surprise. "Daddy!"

"Baby, why are you naked?"

Jolene scrambled in search of her nightgown. She found it in a ball near the top of the bed on the floor. As she bent to pick it up, a metallic pouch gleamed from the wastebasket. Suddenly, she became acutely aware of her condition in front of her father. She slipped her nightgown over her head all the while demurring.

"I'm sorry, Daddy. It was so hot in here during the night and I was too lazy to get up to turn the heat down. Jolene slid herself to the bottom of the bed to draw her father's attention from near the wastebasket.

"What are you doing home? I wasn't expecting you until tomorrow sometime."

"I left early. The Council was arguing over whether to accept LGBT clergy into the ministry. It was very clear the issue was not going to get resolved, so I left. I'm not terribly sure we should be having that conversation anyway. The Bible is pretty clear about it."

"Oh, Daddy, you are so old-fashioned. Maybe it's not so vile after all?"

Rev. Young winced, "I've gotta pee like a Russian racehorse. I didn't stop at the airport restroom and I was too embarrassed to ask the Uber driver. He exited the room and Jolene could hear him urinating from down the hall.

While relieving himself, Rev. Young noticed a strange hair on the rim of the toilet. What is that? He tore off a piece of toilet paper and collected the evidence like a detective on *Law & Order*. He examined the tissue closely for a few moments. Pretty sure he knew what the strange hair was, Young went back to his daughter's room. "Jolene, was that boy here?" Her father's rancor startled Jolene.

"Who? What boy? No, Daddy. Nobody was here."

"Are you sure?"

"Yes, Daddy. Nobody was here. Why do you ask?" Jolene's worried her nervousness would reveal her concealed truth.

Rev. Young scanned the room. "Oh, it's just a feeling." While her father glanced about, Jolene slyly stretched her foot to overturn the wastebasket . A dull ache between her legs reminded her of a comment she had made to Nahim as he danced naked in the moonlight. She had declared "You're not putting that baseball bat inside me."

"Hmph... Maybe it's time I meet Nahim?" Rev. Young wanted to believe his daughter, but doubts remained.

Chapter 22

Responding to the doorbell's chime, Jolene nervously sighed as she stood up. She and her father had been sitting on the couch discussing Nahim's arrival. "Daddy, promise me you'll be nice to him."

Rev. Young also stood. His Cheshire grin belied his affirmation.

"Daddy....be on your best behavior."

"Get the door, silly. I ain't gonna hurt that boy." Rev. Young smoothed his slacks and straightened his cardigan as he prepared to receive his guest. He looked at his watch on his left wrist. "He's punctual. That's a good sign."

Jolene smiled as she swung the door open on its hinges. "Hey, baby, c'mon in." Nahim's tall frame filled the doorway. "Daddy, this is Nahim. Nahim, my daddy."

With outstretched hand, Nahim deferred, "It's a pleasure to meet you, Mister Young."

"That's Reverend or Pastor Young," Jolene's dad strongly interrupted. The bass in his voice suggested to Nahim this would be a more formal exchange rather than the easy conversation Jolene had promised.

"I'm sorry. Rev. Young."

"Please, come in." Rev. Young postured an invitation to the living room sofa. "It's so nice to finally meet you. Jolene talks about you all the time." Rev. Young sat in his chair, a wing-back that made him look like a king holding audience at court. " Something to drink?"

No thank you, sir." Nahim dry swallowed as he watched the reverend pour a tall glass of lemonade. The ice in the glass sparkled as the liquid nestled between the cracks between the ice cubes. Nahim's nerves tingled as he watched the satisfaction of the cool liquid ease down Rev. Young's throat.

After a satiated "Aah" Rev. Young began, "Nahim, thank you for coming today. I can remember what it felt like meeting Jolene's grandparents the first time. I was a bundle of nerves." Nahim chuckled as Young continued. "I don't want to take too much of your time. Let's get down to business, shall we?"

Nahim took note of the large print family Bible displayed on the coffee table and the statue of Jesus hanging on the cross above the archway—droplets of blood trickling down Jesus's forehead. The statue appeared oddly staged above Rev. Young's throne.

"Nahim, what are your intentions toward my daughter?"

Surprised by the first question of the conversation, Nahim choked out an answer. "Well, sir, I am quite fond of Jolene," Nahim glanced at his girl who anxiously knelt at the coffee table. He reached out and playfully tugged at Jolene's hair, which seemed to ease the tension (at least hers). The corners of Jolene's mouth turned upward. Nahim happened to see Rev. Young's slight scowl at the intimacy the teens expressed.

"Well, Nahim, I happen to be in a weird position here. I am Jolene's dad, but I am also her pastor—both roles I take very seriously. As her pastor, I have to consider the condition of her spiritual life." He paused perhaps to emphasize the profundity of the statement.

"Nahim, I have to ask, how would you characterize your relationship with God?"

"Dad. You promised." Jolene's curtness suggested Rev. Young had crossed a predetermined line of discussion.

When it seemed less tense, Nahim inserted, "I'm not perfect, but God loves me anyway."

"So true. His grace and mercy is amazing for sure."

Later, as he departed the Youngs' house, Nahim innocently kissed Jolene's cheek under Rev. Young's watchful eye. Nahim didn't breathe again until his feet hit the concrete of the sidewalk. Jolene joined him and together they walked to the bus stop. There she gave him a proper kiss before Nahim entered the bus.

Jolene breathed a sigh of relief figuring Nahim had passed the first hurdle. She closed the front door behind her. When she turned around smiling, her father appeared, arms crossed, "I don't like him."

Jolene whined, "Why, Daddy?"

"The Bible says 'Don't be unequally yoked.' You should not be with him." His matter of fact tone energized his disapproval.

"Unequally yoked? What are you talking about? We're not that different."

"He's elusive. He never once looked me in the eye. That means he's hiding something. Worse, he never answered that spiritual question. He looked like a deer caught in headlights. I'm not even sure he knew what I was talking about."

"He probably couldn't talk because you were being so hard on him. Daddy, Nahim is a good guy. He loves Jesus and he loves me. That's all that matters."

"That's not all that matters. He's got the devil in him. I don't want you seeing that boy anymore."

Chapter 23

"Nahim, I'm going to fail this midterm. I feel so stupid!" Jolene held her head in her hands as she sat at her kitchen table."

"You're not stupid. Don't cut yourself down like that." Nahim stood behind Jolene's chair rubbing her shoulders. Head turned sideways to feign supportive, Nahim kneaded her flesh. He threw in a few soft swipes to her long, brown hair for good measure. "Babe, you just need to calm down. Your midterm isn't for another week."

"I just don't get this Chemistry stuff. We've been learning this stuff for the last several months, so a week isn't very reassuring. And just when am I actually going to get a chance to study? I've got student council after school on Tuesdays and Thursdays. Youth group on Wednesdays. Diversity Club, FBLA, and Care Club. Not to mention I have homework and tests in my other classes. I just can't do this!" A tiny tear welled up in the corner of Jolene's eye. Exasperated, Jolene forcefully pushed her chemistry book off the table. Her notebook flew too. The pages clapped as it launched. The thud echoed throughout the room. "And when am I ever going to get to see you? When am I ever going to use this stuff? The chair scrunched on the hardwood floor when Jolene backed up to retrieve her books. "Look at this mess!" She flipped through her spiral notebook. "Stoichiometry, equilibrium, acids and bases. Who cares? I'm never going to need to know this again!"

"You've got this babe. I believe in you." Trying to lighten the mood and quell her frustration, Nahim blurted, "Somebody's got a birthday coming up this weekend." He asked what she wanted in a sing-song.

Loudly, "I want a good grade on this friggin' midterm! If I fail, my dad is going to freak out. I'll get the 'God calls us to excellence speech' again. Hear this Reverend Young, I don't need to hear that we are the *ecclesia*—the called-out ones—again!" Jolene pantomimed how she'd maybe fuss with her dad.

That weekend, Nahim had kept this exchange in his mind; Nahim presented Jolene with a birthday present—a gift certificate to Buoyant, a new day spa in the area. "You and I are going on a date so you can relax. We're going to go floating."

"Floating? What's that?" Her face quizzical.

"Just what I said—floating. It's a relaxation spa. We're going to float. It's supposed to be super healthy. An hour float, then we'll get a couples massage. I have already scheduled it and paid for it; so, you're going."

"Oh, 'Him, you're so thoughtful. Thank you so much. I've never had a massage before." Jolene began to tear up in gratitude. She took a light hop and landed a quaint kiss on Nahim's lips. When they arrived at Buoyant, Jolene's excitement radiated from her grinning smile. The spa was situated in a little house just off the main drag. The pair were greeted by Lisa, a petite Asian (probably Filipino) woman who welcomed them to Buoyant. Lisa instructed them to remove their shoes and place them in the provided lockers. She then gave them a tour of the facilities. "I was going to ask if either of you had been here before, but I remember you from when you made this appointment, right?" Lisa's memory impressed Nahim.

"Yup, that was me. But, I've never done this. Just made the appointment."

"OK. I think you'll love it." Lisa led the duo through a couple back hallways. She paused at a cozy space with a couple of couches. "When you're done, you can just relax in this room until your partner is ready. Then, Rock will come and get your for your bodywork massage. Follow me." She continued to the last room on the right. "This will be your room." When I leave," she told Jolene, you should take a shower and then get into this isolation tank." Lisa opened the door of the tank to further explain how floating works.

"This is a sensory deprivation tank, also called an isolation tank. It's used is used for restricted environmental stimulation therapy (or REST). It is a dark, soundproof tank that is filled with a foot or less of salt water. There are over 1200 pounds of salt in there, so when you get in, just lay back and rest. The tank will do

the work. You have an unlimited float period. Take your time. It'll
be dark in there. Try not to get any of the water in your mouth or
eyes. When you're done, please take another shower." She pointed out the soap, shampoo, and conditioner dispensers on the wall.
"There's a toilet right there if you need one. Enjoy. You, sir, are
coming to the next room." Nahim dutifully followed.

"Hey," He turned back to Jolene, "Relax and try to forget
about midterms. Have a good time, honey."

"Oh, I will. Thank you so much, babe. You are so thoughtful."

When Nahim was out of sight, Jolene removed her clothes
and put on the special ear plugs Lisa provided. She turned the
shower on and was tremendously thankful for the powerful water
pressure.

"I could just stay in this shower for the whole time." When
she'd finally finished, she made sure to pee first before getting
into the tank. She ducked as she descended into the shallow tank.
She actually slipped on the slick flooring and made a big splash.
She reached backwards to close the tank door. She tried her hard-
est to immediately begin relaxing in the darkness, but that was
challenging as she deeply regretted shaving earlier that morning.
When she awoke from napping, she had no idea what time it was
nor how long she had been asleep. "I didn't know I was so tired.
Let me get out of here. Nahim's probably waiting. She yawned and
stretched before exiting the tank. She again found the after shower as tranquilizing as the previous. She dried herself in the big
towel Lisa had left in the room and slowly put her clothes back on.
She was correct. Nahim patiently waited for her in the relaxation
room. "Oh, hey, babe. How was it?

"Ah-mazing! There are no words. Wait, there are two
words. That shower."

"I know, right!" Jolene sat next to him on the couch exhal-
ing as she let her head rest on the back cushion."

"Oh my goodness. I feel so good."

Lisa appeared in the room. "Just wait until Rock works out
the kinks. You guys ready?"

Jolene elated, "I am. C'mon, babe."

"You don't have to call me twice." He stood up and adjusted

his basketball shorts.

Lisa led them back out front and to the right. They reached Rock's area who instructed them to undress to their level of comfort and get face down underneath the sheets before he left the room.

"My partner's name is Helonika. Do you guys care which of us is your therapist?"

"I don't care. Nahim?"

"I'll take Helonika. No offense, Rock. You understand, right?"

As Rock closed the door behind him, Nahim began to completely undress.

"Wait. You're getting naked?"

"HE said undress to our level of comfort. I'm comfortable being naked."

"I don't know if I want some strange woman rubbing all over your naked body."

"Oh, relax, babe. It'll be fine."

Nahim regretted his ease of thinking he'd be ok with Rock making Jolene singing Rock's praises and his magic hands within earshot. Particularly when she exclaimed, "Oh yeah, right there. Harder!"

When the timer dinged signaling the end of their massage time, Jolene lifted her head from the pillow. "Oh, thank you, Rock. SO GOOD! Nahim, you sounded like you got a good nap." "Girl, I was out. Thanks, Helonika. It was great."
The couple dressed and returned to the back room. Lisa stood in the kitchen rinsing her coffee mug. "SO, how was your first floating experience?'

Jolene gushed, "I found myself very relaxed during my 2nd float. I was able to see clearly that the "stuff" in my life was keeping me from being my true self. I visualized removing clutter from my life, room by room in the tank. I felt prepared to tackle the challenges of the school year. It was wonderful. It is amazing what you can feel, clear and then accomplish when your brain takes you on this floating experience. This was my first float experience but will not be my last!"

"Good. That's what we like to hear."

Chapter 24

"Who can tell me who was known as 'the mother of the Civil Rights Movement'?"

"That's an easy one." Lexi confidently answered "Rosa Parks."

"That's right. But why do we know her? What is she famous for?"

"She didn't give up her seat on the bus."

"True, but say more." Davis had a sneaky look on his face. I think I'll stay quiet and watch these white people try their luck.

"She refused to give up her seat to a white man on a bus in Montgomery, Alabama, even though she knew the law said she was supposed to go to the back of the bus. Her arrest started the Montgomery Bus Boycott." *Wipe that smug look off your face. You got one answer right this whole year. Now you think you did something.*

"*Good job, Alexis. Who was Claudette Colvin?" Ooh, that shut you up, huh?* Dr. Davis waited in silence for others to chime in. When no one else did, he continued his lecture.

"And that's my point. It's Black History Month, and we all know who Rosa Parks was. American education has failed us. Let me teach you some real black history. Your history teachers have probably taught the five second version of black history: Black folks arrived in chains, Abraham Lincoln set us free, Rosa Parks, Martin Luther King, Jr., now Obama. Sound about right?" *Exactly.*

"Claudette Colvin should be a recognizable name, but yet, she's not. Here's why you should know her. Claudette was riding a Montgomery public bus from school. Like Mrs. Parks, Claudette refused to give up her seat and was arrested--nine months BEFORE Rosa Parks. What I'm interested in knowing is why Rosa? Why not Claudette? Thoughts?" Dumbfounded looks all around.

"Could it be that it was because Claudette was just 15 years old when she decided to assert her rights? Or was it because she had a reputation for being considered her to be too 'feisty', 'emotional' and 'mouthy' to be a good symbol for the bus boycotts? In Claudette's own words 'My mother told me to be quiet about what I did,' Colvin said. "She told me to let Rosa be the one: white people aren't going to bother Rosa, they like her." Or, could it be that we have a hero worship culture, especially related to American Civil Rights? I am not meaning to disparage Mother Rosa, but I want to give respect to Sister Claudette as well. For every Rosa there's an unsung Claudette. For every Martin King a Mose Wright. For every Olaudah Equiano, an enslaved cook named Judah on some plantation in Virginia. All people who deserve to be remembered. Mrs. Parks had a really good reputation as a warrior for the struggle. I remember watching some documentary years ago where someone said 'If they could do this to Mrs. Parks, they could do it to any of us.'

"That's what galvanized the people to commit to walking for the next 364 days. The Montgomery Bus Boycott was possibly the most effective protest and social action of the 20th century. Those ordinary folks—janitors, porters, plumbers, and garbage-men gave their time and pledged with their bodies to walk miles to and from work every single day in Alabama weather to end the injustice. Imagine, all inspired by a 15-year-old girl. In a way, Claudette has been forgotten—ignored by history simply because of American hero worship."

"What do you mean-hero worship?"

"Well, Violet think about it. When you think about any-thing related to civil rights in America, what is the first name that comes to mind?"

Smiling, Violet proudly retorted, "Reverend Dr. Martin Luther King."

"Exactly my point. We've become obsessed with Dr. King. An important man, no doubt, but I can't help but think about the struggles and accomplishments of the ordinary folks who launched the Civil Rights Movement. Ever since King's death, we've been waiting for the next Dr. King. After his speech at the DNC in 2004, people kept calling Obama 'the next MLK' and encouraged him to run for senate and for the presidency in 2008. I'm going to go out on a limb here and say we don't need to wait for 'the next Martin Luther King. He's long been dead.

"Hear what Dr. King's own daughter says." Davis read from a typed paper, 'Don't act like everyone loved my father. He was assassinated. A 1967 poll reflected that he was one of the most hated men in America. Most hated. Many who quote him now and evoke him to deter justice today would likely hate, and may already hate, the authentic King.' "That's Rev Dr. Berneice A. King, Dr. King's youngest daughter.

"Some of you may be under the false assumption that the quest for Civil Rights ended when Dr. King was murdered, but the fight continues. Until we have equal rights for all under the law, the fight continues. I'm not calling for the next anyone. But I do think the world is waiting for Lexie Borja, for Didrik Anchorstar, yes, even you Mr. Lightbourne. I see you hiding behind Westley, Will you be next to stand up, to fight for the rights of others, to put yourself in a sacrificial posture for the sake of the poor, the only, the needy, the castaway? I believe that any one of you," as he pointed around the room, " has greatness inside of you, has the ability to inspire others to be the difference that someone else needs.

As he preached, Dr. Davis made eye contact with each of his students. When he called a name, his mention seemed to incite a spark in their eyes. Even more so, his chest seemed to swell with pride as he cheered his charges. His pace slowed, and he stopped walk-talking in front of the television. He pressed play on the DVD player. The music introducing *Eyes on the Prize* filled the room: "I know the one thing we did right was the day we started to fight.

Keep your eyes on the prize, hold on."

The black & white footage set the stage. We were going back in time. The documentary began to focus on the murder of Emmit Till. Nahim's heart broke as he watched Mamie Till-Bradley share the pain of losing her 14-year-old son all because he dared to whistle at a pretty white girl. Nahim's thoughts turned towards Jolene. He felt guilty for being in love with a white girl.

The next day, the classroom filled the same way it had all semester. Dr. Davis greeted, "Good morning class." Walking towards the DVD stand, "We're going to pick up where we left off yesterday with *Eyes on the Prize*. When class ended, the citizens of Montgomery, Alabama had just celebrated the Supreme Court's declaration that the segregated bus system was unconstitution- al. Today, we'll pick up with the battle for integrated schools. He turned his back to the class to walk towards the TV.

Westley interrupted. "Doctor Davis, before you press play, can I ask a question?"

"Sure, go ahead. Inquiry is an essential part of learning."

"Why do we always have to talk about race?"

"We don't always talk about race."

"Tsk. Sure we do. Don't we y'all?" He sought for affirma- tion from the other students.

A few chimed in, "Yes, we do." and "For real."

"Alright, Alright. I admit it. We do talk about race quite a bit. But this is American Studies, right?"

Westley bandied, "Dude, but all this black talk is pretty heavy. Why do I have to come to school to be made to feel guilty. My ancestors didn't own slaves. Why do you want to make us feel bad."

Turning his head to the side, Dr. Davis insisted, "Westley, I don't want you to feel bad. If you feel bad, maybe there's some- thing you need to understand about yourself?" He turned his back as he suggested that question. I saw that sarcastic smile, sir. "You see, race and racism are coded into the American fabric. You'd might say, we perfected it." Turning to Westley, "Westley, a few moments ago, you defended that your ancestors didn't own slaves. I wonder if you've ever traced your family ancestry to veri- fy that? America , for instance, perfected slavery."

"Doc, Africans sold other Africans into slavery."

"That is true. Slavery is nothing new. Almost every country in the world practiced slavery, but slavery in other nations was primarily related to being a prisoner of war or through indebt- edness." Pausing, "Has anyone heard of the term 'indentured servant?' "Indentured servitude was akin to slavery. If you were indebted to me, you were basically my slave—for a specific time period until such time as the debt was paid. Americans were the ones who made the trade about race. It was about genetics and capitalism. By making slavery about skin color, that policy cod- ified the intergenerational nature of slavery. The law said, the

child follows the condition of the mother. If the mother was enslaved, all of her children were too. Think about this for a second.
Why do you think so many slaveowners raped and impregnated
their enslaved women?"

Just then Violet chimed in. "Dr. Davis, why has no one ever
taught us this stuff?"

"You tell me. I have some ideas, but it would be better if
you came up with them on your own. I will say, though, this country would be nothing without the institution of slavery." American
history, economics, politics, government, even criminal justice
and old fashioned juris prudence all have the stench of slavery on
them."

"But, you act like I'm Bull Connor or something. You need
to get over it."

Davis struck by the admission glared in Nahim's direction.
"Oh so you know who Bull Connor was?"

Chapter 25

The lights lowered in the classroom for yet another install-ment of *Eyes on the Prize*.

Westley began, "Oh please, Doc, do we have to watch this? I can't take it anymore.

"Yes, we do. And I think you can handle it."

Westley huffed aloud. "Seriously, though, Doc. I know you think all white people are racists, but I am starting to think that maybe you are the racist one?"

Davis joked. "I can't be racist. Some of my best friends are white." Davis waited for the joke to land. "Westley thinks I'm racist. Well, I'm gonna ignore that comment right now, but I promise to circle back to it. For now, sit back. Relax. We're pick-ing up the story in 1965." Davis pressed play.

The narrator began setting the stage for the content of the episode—voting rights. The footage showed a very young Martin Luther King receiving the Nobel Peace Prize for his stalwart in-sistence on using peaceful, nonviolent resistance as a method to quell the hatred turned at American Negroes.

The documentary continued. At about fifteen minutes in, the discussion began to address the killing of Jimmie Lee Jackson as he tried to protect his mother from attack during a nighttime march in Marion, Alabama. Jimmie had been killed by an Alabama state trooper.

"UGH! Y'all been killin' us forever!"

"Nahim, please." Davis urged Nahim against blurting out. Pallbearers carried Jimmie's flower-topped casket into a church while mourners sang the familiar song "We Shall Overcome." Soon, Martin Luther King, Jr.'s voice emphasized, "He was mur-dered by the irresponsibility of every politician from governors on down who has fed his constituents the stale bread of hatred and the spoiled meat of racism. He was murdered by the timidity of a federal government that can spend millions of dollars a day to keep troops in South Vietnam and cannot protect the lives of its own citizens seeking the right to vote."

The archival footage moved towards the ceremonial 54-mile march from Selma to Montgomery. When the footage showed the title of the Edmund Pettus Bridge in Montgomery, Davis paused the DVD.

"Westley suggests that I am racist. I'm assuming he feels that way because, to date, the documentary has primarily highlighted only the negative things white folks have done. Well, that all changes here at Edmund Pettus. I'll warn you, the next part of this is hard to watch. It's quite graphic and violent. In fact, the march across the bridge is referred to in the history books as 'Bloody Sunday.' Remember, at this time, national broadcast television is a relatively young and new medium. The national media was on hand. The violence perpetuated against white participants, allies really, captured by the news cameras is what galvanized the consciousness of the white populace across America."

Once Davis unpaused, the marchers continued across the bridge. Waiting on the other side was an army of Alabama state troopers on horseback—gasmasks on--guns and batons drawn. One officer using a bullhorn barked "It will be detrimental to your safety to continue this march, and I'm saying it is an unlawful assembly. You have to disperse. Go home or go to your church. This march will not continue." The marchers—most with their hands in their pockets—did not comply and the wall of officers advanced and began antagonizing and pushing the protestors. Bedlam ensued as the men, women, and children were beaten senselessly. It wasn't long before tear gas bombs resounded and smoke filled the air.

Several statesmen and government officials offered castigation towards Governor Wallace's callousness. They admitted the marchers posed no threat to the public safety of the city. They would argue the inappropriate level of the officers' response. A white Texas Senator, Ralph Yarbourough, offered a scathing rebuke, "Shame on you, George Wallace, for the wet ropes that bruised the muscles, for the bull whips that cut the flesh, for the clubs that broke the bones, for the teargas that seared the eyes, the nose, the nostrils, the lungs, and choked people into insensibility. This is not the American way!"

"Bullshit!" Nahim roiled. "This is exactly the American way when it comes to black folks."

"Oh, shut up, Nahim! Keep your nigger mouth shut!" Logan seemed as exasperated as Nahim. His pubescent voice cracked. "Who the hell you think you're talking to? Yo, Wes, you best come get ya boy before he gets hurt!" Nahim postured towards Logan. The documentary turned attention towards an older Yarborough who admitted "When this happened in Selma, and I saw it on television, to me it expanded beyond civil rights, beyond whether you vote, or where you sit in a restaurant, where you sit in a café or on planes, train, or buses, it became a matter of human life—an issue that transcended any of those we were voting on." In short order, the mood of the documentary shifted to the presence of 450 white clergymen who arrived in Selma from across the country to stand in solidarity with those in Selma struggling for the right to vote. Buoyed by the support, a second march was called for Tuesday. The protestors had increased from 600 to 2,000. The police presence had increased also. Rev. Ralph Abernathy, a compatriot of King's, prayed and reminded those attending "Cause we know that America was founded upon the principles that all men were created equal. Not just white men, but all men. After the prayer, Dr. King led the group back over the bridge but discontinued the march to avoid a potential repeat of the Sunday melee.

As King and the other marchers made their retreat, several police officers followed and began assaulting the marchers. Reverend James Kreeb, a white minister was killed. "Isn't it interesting," Davis interrupted, "I t didn't bother anyone that police were killing black people, but when a white person was victimized, there was a great national outcry? You see, Westley, I do believe there were and are some good white people committed to the cause. For instance, one of my heroes of the movement was Viola Liuzzo."

"Who is that?" Nahim did not bother to look up to see who had asked the question. He wrung his hands—his nostrils swollen in anger.

"You don't know the name Viola Liuzzo? I'm not surprised.

She isn't very well known or venerated, but she should be. She drove all the way from Detroit to Selma to support the march. She drove all night because she wanted to do her part. She helped to shuttle marchers to and from various events and mass meetings. One fateful day, late in the evening, she was driving alone on a Selma highway after driving several marchers around, four members of the Ku Klux Klan drove alongside of her car and shot her. 39 years old, married, mother of 5. She died for what she believed in. It has been said that before she was shot, she had gotten her car up to 100 miles an hour trying to escape. One of the accused killers admitted she had looked directly at them before she was shot. Viola Liuzzo. May she rest in power." Davis lowered his head and raised a Black Power fist.

"Oh my God! That is horrible. Why haven't we heard this before?" Lexie cried out.

"You tell me, Lexie. Why do you think you've never heard this story?"

Nervous to answer, Lexie sheepishly mumbled, "Um, because they want us to think only black people should be concerned about Civil Rights?"

Davis loudly clapped his hands together in affirmation. "That's right! And I could list several others white martyrs who died in the struggle that we should celebrate. Great job, Lex. You're learning how systems of power and oppression work." Davis smiled wide his characteristic grin--pride glowing. He took his seat and restarted the DVD.

The video continued showing a verbal altercation between a police officer and a group of college-aged blacks attempting to walk to the courthouse to pray. The officer referred to the students as "niggers" multiple times. It was when the officer explained that he did not believe in "equal justice," but in "justice" and described the black student as not worthy of equal treatment, Nahim with crocodile tears in his eyes, said "Goddammit, I hate you sons-of-bitches." Standing from his desk, Nahim picked up his large textbook and approached Logan from behind. "Who are you calling a nigger, Pecker Wood?" He slammed his textbook at the base of Logan's neck. The sheer force of the blow slammed

Logan's head forward where his forehead and bridge of his nose ricocheted off the desk.

When Logan picked his head up, blood spurted from his nose. Nahim stood over the crooked neck of his victim. "I bet you won't call me a nigger again! Logan's eyes were already blackening. Seeing this, Dr. Davis yelled, "Quick, somebody go get the school nurse!"

Chapter 26

"I want that little..." Walking in the office door, Mrs. Potter stopped short of the n-word when she noticed Nahim sitting in the corner before continuing her rant, "black boy arrested for attempted murder!" She had requested a meeting with the headmaster first thing Monday morning.

"That's a little extreme, Mrs. Potter. Nahim wasn't trying to kill him."

"Oh no, don't you dare try to minimize this! He almost killed my boy. From the way Logan told me, Nahim threatened to hurt him in front of this Dr. Davis 'class." Look at him. Poor Logan looked pitiful in a neck brace—both eyes blackened—the swelling looked like it was just beginning to go down.

"The doctors said if that book had hit him just two inches to the left, Logan would probably be paralyzed or dead. He was just shy of hitting his cerebellum. You should have heard the laundry list of what-ifs: loss of coordination of motor movement, the inability to judge distance and when to stop, the inability to perform rapid alternating movements, movement tremors, staggering, wide based walking, tendency toward falling, weak muscles, slurred speech, and, abnormal eye movements."

She listed each condition matter-of-factly. "I had to help him get a shower. I had to help him get dressed this morning. Logan lowered his head in shame. "My poor baby."

"Your poor baby called my son a nigger!" Mrs. Lightbourne practically jumped from her chair.

"Oh, he would never do that. I've taught him better than that."

"He said it in front of Dr. Davis' class." Nahim defended. "It wasn't the first time either."

"See, in front of the entire class?' Mrs. Lightbourne chimed in.

Headmaster Williams questioned "If that's true, Nahim,

why didn't you react this way before?"

"It happens all the time. I'm sorry. I just blew up. Maybe it was just the timing? We'd been watching that documentary in class about the Civil Rights Movement."

"Isn't this Doctor Davis the one who we'd had problems with before? He's a troublemaker." Looking at the headmaster, "We've never had problems like this before you hired him." Nahim suddenly became aware that he might be getting Dr. Davis into trouble, so he stopped talking. He refused to speak anymore preferring to let the adults carry the bulk of the conversation. He even managed to keep his mouth shut when Mrs. Potter dogged Dr. Davis' teaching methods. In fact, Nahim phased out while the parents talked. When he tuned back in, the headmaster was beginning to wrap up the meeting.

Adjusting the stack of papers on his desk, Headmaster Williams added, "Well, we'll ask Dr. Davis to share his version of the goings on in his classroom on the fateful day. I am sure he has a particular view of what transpired." Satisfied that the papers were sufficiently stacked, Headmaster Williams gestured to allow the women space to exit his office.

"Mrs. Potter, don't you worry."
"I wonder if we need to get this issue before the board? If you don't do something, maybe we'll have to find a new headmaster? Williams acquiesced. He grinned at Logan and cajoled, "Stay healthy, Tiger. Get back to us soon. Mr. Lightbourne, you go on and get to second period.

Second period. Dr. Davis' class. I'll admit it. I grinned a little on the inside. I wasn't excited about returning to the scene of the crime as it were, but I enjoyed Davis' class more than any of my other classes. I think I actually learned something. I stopped at my locker en route so I could at lease look prepared. I grabbed a pen and my textbook. The book felt heavier than it did on Friday. I opened the door slowly—my plan being to simply slide into a rear seat without causing a stir.

"There he is. Na-heem!" I hadn't seen anyone since the altercation on Friday. I fronted to the fellas and signified to a few others. I didn't want them to know I almost killed Logan.

"Yo! I saw Logan's mom in the parking lot. Man, she looked

rough!" Didrik leaned over to add his piece, "Man, I heard Logan is JACKED UP!" I don't know what came over me.

"I guess that's the last time he parts his lips to call me a nigger!"

"Damn, yo! That's tough!"

"Damn, Na'. Westley reached over to give some dap.

Dr. Davis stood at the board and continued his lecture. The words WHEN DID THE CIVIL RIGHTS MOVEMENT END? scrawled on the board.

I didn't see Jolene until the end of the day. When I saw her first, a deep cavern jelled inside my belly. I felt overcome by fear and shame. I hadn't seen her since all the hullaballoo went down and I knew she'd ask too many questions, have too many inquiries. Totally not in the mood to be peppered with questions.

"Hey babe." My lips barely grazed hers as we quickly embraced.

"Hey. How are you? I feel like I haven't seen you in forever. How was your weekend?"

She hadn't heard? How did she get away with not hearing? Grabbing her close, Nahim slipped his arms around the small of Jolene's back and squeezed. AT the same time, he exhaled deeply. "Oh, baby, it's been crazy. I'm so glad to see your face. His hot breath on her neck caused goosebumps to trickle down her arms. Nahim gave Jolene a nice squeeze hug. It was as if he left a huge weight at her feet. Jolene felt a teardrop connect with the side of her neck. She took a step backward and asked, "Are you crying?" She wiped her cheek with her right hand to inspect the source of wetness. She grabbed Nahim's face in her hands so she could get a better look. 'Baby, what's wrong?"

Nahim struggled with telling Jolene the truth of the past few days or being stoically masculine and keeping it all inside. In moments, he poured his heart out on Jolene's shoulder. "Oh, babe. It's so sad. I lost it. I lost it.

"Lost it? Lost what? What happened?

Between tears, Nahim mumbled, "Logan. Logan. I lost it." He composed himself long enough to finish his confession. "Logan called me a nigger and I almost killed him."

"What? When did this happen?" Jolene quizzed.

"Friday in Dr. Davis' class."

"Friday? And I'm just hearing about it now?"

" I didn't want to bother you with this stupid nonsense."
Jolene grabbed Nahim's face with both of her hands. "Babe, listen
to me. You are never a bother to me. You are not in this alone. It's
me and you. Besides, this is important. Now, tell me what happened."

Nahim did just that. He emptied his heart as he retold
the events of the incident. "I don't know what happened. I just
snapped! I admit to having been in my feelings having watched
that documentary and for Logan to be so carelessly flip and call me
out my name just wasn't smart. Before I knew anything, he was
bleeding everywhere, and I was on my way to the office."

"OMG! That's crazy babe." She slid his New York Yankees
cap from his head and buried her fingers deep in Nahim's coarse
locks. She stroked and caressed his head and whispered her support into his ears.

A few moments later, Nahim perked up and suggested they
go home. "I've been at this school all day. Let's go."

Chapter 27

"It's all my fault.' Dr. Davis held his head in his hands and rocked back and forth. "I should have known. Should have seen it."

"Zeke, how could you have known Nahim would freak out like that?" Lisa put her hand softly on Dr. Davis' shoulder and tried to assuage his apparent guilt.

Davis repeated, "I should have seen it coming. I should have known. Lisa," he lifted his head, "you should have seen how those kids treated him. I mean, he's way stronger than I am. I would have snapped out long before this. He just took it. He swallowed it all. And, I just kept pushing. I had something to prove to those white folks. I should have left it alone."

"You couldn't have known. Nahim is a private person. He doesn't tell everyone his feelings or what he's going through."

"Lisa, I should have known. Brother James said, 'To be a Negro in this country and to be relatively conscious is to be in a state of rage almost all of the time.' Add, Nahim and I have been reading conscious black authors and debating what it means to be black in the United States." He looked directly into Lisa's eyes as tears filled his own, "I just wanted him to feel good about being black... to find some strength in who he was. He, like many black students I've come across, had accepted the idea that all black people in America are descended from slaves. But what if they understood themselves as victors and survivors rather than as weak victims?" I always told him 'Every good soup begins with good stock.'

"That school needs more good teachers like you." Lisa hoped her encouragement would bolster Thaddeus' negative mood.

"That's true. They need several. Especially since I won't be there anymore."

"What are you talking about? Where are you going?"

"They fired me. They're blaming my teaching on Nahim's outburst. They won't admit their 'innocent little boys and girls' are racist devils. Of course, turn a blind eye to their discriminatory acts towards Nahim, but as soon as the black boy stands up for himself, he's Public Enemy #1. And, then, sacrifice their first and only black teacher. Headmaster Williams told me Logan's mother was circulating a petition among the other parents asking the board punish Williams for not stepping in to censure my teaching."

"Oh, Zeke, I am so sorry. I should have never let the boy go to that school. He should have stayed at Hughes. Try as I might to raise them right. A lot of good that has done. He's still setting in a jail cell."

"Lisa, The white man has been after Nahim for a long time. Did you know they track black boys in what's called the school-to-prison pipeline? Black students are suspended or expelled three times more frequently than white students. And while black children made up 16 percent of all enrolled children, according to federal data, they accounted for 31 percent of all in-school arrests. Taking him out of the public school was probably the best thing you could have done. Nahim is a gifted boy; that school could have never supported him, never encouraged his gifts. He's on the verge of being the valedictorian of his class and going off to UVA on a full scholarship. That is huge! The statistics are even worse for black boys whose fathers are not in the home."

"Damn Monarch! Zeke, I love that you have been there for Nahim. Thank you for speaking into his life. Yes, he is in a bad situation right now, but he can't lose you." She quieted , swallowing hard, "I can't lose you." Lisa stepped forward, grabbing Thaddeus' face, and kissed him slowly and passionately.

Taken aback by her kiss, Thaddeus, pulled back. He asked, "Lisa, what are you doing?"

"Zeke, I'm trying to show you, to tell you I love you. These past few months since you've been in our lives have been some of my greatest times since Monarch left. I remember that first day I saw you at the school. You were up on that stage and were telling them white folks what they wasn't gonna do. I sat in the back of that auditorium feeling like a schoolgirl with a crush. And now, you've been like a father to Nahim. I love you for that."

"You're a great mom. You've done a good job with those boys—all of them. Even Tyreek. As much as we try, we've got to allow them to make their own choices. Sure, it gets hard. My mom used to say she could teach us many things, but she couldn't teach my brothers and me to be a man...And I love you, too. It's weird, when Amy left me, I didn't think I'd find love again, but these last few months with you all has taught me the hope and importance of having a family. Truth be told, though, we were a match made in hell, though. My therapist told me that I'm dismissive/avoidant attachment style and she was anxious attachment style. That meant that she needed a lot more attention than I was willing or able to give. She'd complain when I'd pack my bags when we'd fight. I never really wanted to leave, but at times, you just need space, you know? But, I have to ask, what do we do about Monarch?"

"What about him? He's been gone a long time, and neither I nor the boys think twice about him. To the boys, he's nothing but a sperm donor, and frankly, to me, he may as well be dead. He moved on, and I would like to also. With you, I hope?"

Thaddeus chuckled and smiled his classic wide-mouthed grin. "Did you just propose to me?"

"I think I did." She paused for a second. "I'm going out to check the mail. Maybe we can talk about that when I come back?" She grabbed her keys from the tabletop. She'd need them to unlock the apartment's mailbox.

Thaddeus stirred his coffee in the mug and sat back deeply in the chair. Soon the front door burst open. Lisa cried hysterically.

" Oh, Zeke, Zeke! They took his scholarship away."

"Who?"

""UVA! Nahim got a letter from them," she shook the letter in Thaddeus' face. "In my curiosity, I opened it. It said, they were notified by Hilton Prep that Nahim was being expelled for assaulting another student and for 'conduct unbecoming a Cavalier' they were rescinding the scholarship and withdrawing their offer of admission. Oh my gawwwd!" Her desperate yawps drove stakes into Thaddeus' heart. He reached out to hug her. He wrapped her up in his big biceps and warmly squeezed. "Zeke, this was just a couple weeks ago. How'd they find out so soon?"

"White people with money. They can make things happen."

"What are we going to do. This news will just kill Nahim!"

Pulling her back into his embrace, "We'll figure out something, together." Lisa pulled back and focused through the teary blur.

"Together." She stood up and refilled her coffee mug. She spooned three healthy scoops of dry cream powder into the mug.

"Have some coffee with your cream?"

"I like it creamy, Zeke."

"I like it when you call me Zeke. Takes me back to the old days on Flatbush Avenue.

"Ooh that was so long ago. Whodathunk we'd reconnect all these years later...in Louisiana, for goodness sakes?
"And that you would propose to me?"

"Well, secretly, I kinda did years ago back in Brooklyn."

"For real? No you didn't."

Lisa blushed and slyly grinned, "No, for real for real. I had the biggest crush on you back then, but we were such close friends, I didn't want to ruin that."

"You neglected to mention you were hung up on Monarch."

With a poor Forrest Gump impression, "Momma always said 'Stupid is as stupid does.' Charge it to my head, but not to my heart. Thank God I've grown up and with age comes wisdom."

"That's true." Thaddeus laughed. "But wait, you were digging me, and I was definitely digging you. How did we never hook up?"

"I don't know. You kinda disappeared once I got pregnant with Tyreek."

Thaddeus explained how he felt like a third wheel and how her getting pregnant was her way of hinting that he would remain in the friend zone. "After a while, you and Monarch were planning your wedding. I took the hint.

"Oh, Zeke. The years I wasted on that man. If we only weren't such young and dumb kids....Kids. Lisa mumbled, "My baby. Nahim...what are we going to do about Nahim?"

"Well, it looks like Hilton has played its first card. We need to talk to a lawyer."

"My, my...look how selfish I'm being. They got my baby down there rotting in some cell and I'm sitting her like a teenager in love."

"I don't think you should worry. He's a minor, so he's in the County lockup, not prison."

Angrily, "I don't care where he is. He's not home with me! Where he should be."

Lisa fixed her hair as she unbound the bus at the stop outside the jail where Nahim was being held. She stopped in front of the rose colored building and emptied her pockets into her purse. The rules posted on the doors indicated her belongings would be put through a metal detector. She didn't want to have the officer putting their hands on her personally.

"Who are you here to see, ma'am?" The officer sat behind a tall station.

"Nahim Lightbourne, sir."

The officer, his badge read Smith, clicked a few keys on the computer in front of him. "Can you spell his first and last name, please?"

"Nahim...N-A-H-I-M, Lightbourne ...L-I-G-H-T-B-O-U-R-N-E."

Smith made a few more clicks on the keyboard. Soon, he turned his chair to the officer to his left." "Sam, I can't find this inmate in the system. Lightbourne?"

"Oh, Lightbourne got transferred to Juvie this morning. He's not here anymore."

"What do you mean he's not here? Shouldn't y'all have notified me? I'm his mother."

"Oh, I'm sorry ma'am. No one called you?"

Defiantly, "Do you think I'd be here if someone had called me? I had to take three buses to get out here. He's a minor. Someone should have called me to let me know where my son was being taken"

"You're right ma'am. Central registration is supposed to do that, but they've been tremendously bogged down. Short staffed, you know. He's across town at the juvenile detention center."

"So, you're saying I came all the way out here for nothing? It took me two hours on that blessed bus, and it'll probably take another two or three to get to the other side of town!"

"Calm down, ma'am. It was a mistake. I'm sorry. But, it's not our fault.

"Don't tell me to calm down. My son is not where he's supposed to be."

"Technically ma'am. He is where he's supposed to be. He probably shouldn't have been brought here on the first place. He's only 17."

"I don't need you, Officer Smith, to tell me how old my son is!"

Lisa huffed and threw her purse overt her shoulder and stormed out of the building.

Chapter 28

"I mean, can you believe that? They didn't even call me. And, after all that, I didn't even get to see him!"

"What? Why?"

"Because by the time I got there, visiting hours were over. I spent the whole day on the bus. Zeke, my baby boy probably thinks I'm not coming to visit him. He's in there all by his lonesome."

"I doubt he thinks that about you, Lisa."

"But, I've always told my boys if they were to get arrested, I was not coming to the jailhouse. Oh, how could they have moved him and not told me?"

"That's probably a good sign. Maybe they're not charging him as an adult?"

Thaddeus went on about how black kids are disproportionately charged as adults. "Typically black boys are seen as men. They are 20 times more likely than white kids to be arrested and charged as adults."

"Oh Zeke. Is that true?"

"Black boys don't typically get to be young. That's reserved for white boys. Black boys are thugs. Black boys are seen as responsible for their actions at an age when white boys still benefit from the assumption that children are essentially innocent. Trayvon Martin, Michael Brown, even Tamir Rice were seen as much older and the pictures released to the press chose to present them as older-looking. Tamir Rice was a baby—just 12 years old when he was gunned down by a cop. I read a study out of UCLA that showed evidence that police officers overestimated the age and culpability of criminals based on racial differences linked to stereotypes. Remember what the media did to Trayvon? They dug up all his old Tweets about him smoking marijuana, but Brock Turner, you know that raped that girl last year. He's known as the "Stanford swimmer" who made a bad decision. Not as a rapist. Black kids they bring up the past. White kids they point to his future. How about that rich white kid down in Texas? He killed four people while drunk and high, and was let off the hook because he complained about his "affluenza." His parents were too rich and never gave him boundaries. Ain't that some shit? The system is jacked, but, maybe Nahim has a shot?"

"I hope so. I guess I'll have to call off work tomorrow to go see him. I'm going to bed."

The following morning, Lisa fixed breakfast for her young sons after she called in sick from her job. A "family emergency" she called it. "Boys, I'm going to visit your brother, Nahim, today."

"Ooh, Mommy, can I go?" Malcolm perked up when she scooped eggs onto his plate.

"Maybe next time. Let me go see how it is first. If it seems okay, I'll try to bring you guys with me. Aunt Jackie is going to pick you up from school, and I'll get there as soon as I can."

That answer seemed to satisfy her youngest sons. Later that morning, she arrived at the Youth Development Center on Frew Mill Road. The bus driver reminded her of the bus's altered schedule. "We've only got one other bus coming out here today. It's the blue line. It'll be here at 2:08 p.m. Lisa thanked the driver and promised to be right outside waiting.

The YDC did not have an armed guard waiting in the front lobby-like at the jail. Instead, an overweight female with dark brown curly hair sat at a reception desk.

"Name," she barked.

Lisa did not know exactly what she was to say, so she hesitated.

"Who do you want to see?"

"Oh, I'm sorry. Nahim Lightbourne, ma'am. Lisa scanned the waiting area. The tan-colored lounge furniture bespoke a dormitory common room not a detention center for delinquents. A white woman wearing burgundy pants and a grey waist jacket patiently waited next to her expensive-looking purse. On the teal couch next to and opposite her sat a middle-aged black man with a greying beard looking at his cell phone. The woman held a calendar in her lap. She kept looking at her watch as if she had been there for a long while. She appeared impatient and agitated. She huffed as she ogled her wrist. Along the rear wall stood a uniformed officer with a clipboard. He was otherwise engaged with a smart-looking white man in a sweater vest.

"Lightbourne, you said, ma'am? What's your relation to the resident?"

"He's my son. I'm his mother."

"Can I see some ID?" Lisa pulled her wallet from her purse and sifted through her credit cards and shopping membership cards until she saw herself. She handed her identification to the desk matron.

Just wait. I'll have him brought down."

Lisa took a seat near the reception area. She crossed her legs as she waited for her son's arrival. While it only took a few minutes, the wait seemed a lifetime.

"Mrs. Lightbourne? Come this way." The rotund desk agent pointed towards a long hallway behind a partially closed door. They passed several windows where residents faced loved ones. They talked on landline phones. She was led past an elderly woman crying and speaking in Spanish. At the fourth window alcove, the desk lady bid Lisa have a seat.

"He'll be brought down shortly. No loud talking. No cursing. Remember all phone calls are being recorded. Have a good visit." She waddled back down the hallway to resume her post.

Lisa sat down on the metal chair and waited for her intended. Moments later, a door opened and Nahim appeared. He was being escorted by a large-sized black man wearing khaki pants and a brown polo shirt. Lisa smiled as her eyes drew in the slight frame of her teen son. Nahim practically jumped at the window when he saw his mother. He slapped the window with his right hand desiring Lisa to touch his hand with hers. With his left hand, he picked up the receiver to the yellow phone in the window. Lisa did the same.

"Hey, baby. How you been? You doing alright?" Lisa teared up. She wanted so badly not to be separated from her son by the heavy pane of glass. She excitedly fired her questions to Nahim.

"You look so thin. Are you eating ok?" Nahim appeared to be swimming in the YDC garb. Lisa grew overwhelmed with emotion.

"Ma, don't cry. I'm OK. How have you been?"

"I've got some bad news, baby." She reached into her purse retrieving the UVA letter. She unfolded it flat and held it up to the window for Nahim to read. "This came for you yesterday." Nahim read through the letter. Tears welled up in his eyes as the realization settled. "Mom, they can't do this! It's not fair!"

"Keep it down, Lightbourne." The khaki-ed man reminded Nahim of the rules.

"How are they treating you in here, son?" Just then, the screams of a male teen rang from the entranceway.

"Mom, these people are crazy. Fights break out all the time. Someone's always screaming."

"Are you getting enough sleep?"

"I'm OK, Mom. I really am. Have you talked to Jolene? How's she doing?"

"Boy, I don't have time to be chasing down your girlfriend. I've been trying to figure out how to get down here to visit your narrow ass."

"I'm sorry. You're right, Mom." Nahim composed himself. "How are Malcolm and Julian?"

"Them boys are running me ragged. They want to come down and see you."

"Mom, no, I don't want them seeing me like this. I can't have them seeing their big brother in here."

Lisa smiled. "You're such a good big brother. My big man."

Chapter 29

As they sat in the court room waiting area, Nahim, Lisa, and Dr. Davis, showed signs of nervousness. Lisa wiped tears, Nahim wiped his sweat, and Thaddeus wrung his hands. They anxiously processed the lawyer's instructions.

"Guys, you're going to have to trust me. No matter what happens in there, I've got your back. Just sit still, no sudden outbursts."

"Oh, Mr. Lamancusa, my nerves are shot. I don't know what this judge is going to say or do."

"Don't worry. The strategy we've planned is going to work."

Thaddeus retorted, "There are no guarantees in juris prudence. It's not criminal justice. It's criminal 'just us.' This is about our boy. He's facing some very real hard time. An attempted murder charge is no light matter—especially against this ofay money."

"I understand, Dr. Davis, but I am just trying to reassure Nahim here that I'm taking this seriously."

Nahim lifted his head in anger, "You better be." He tugged at his shirt. "I still wish you had fought harder for me to be able to wear a real suit and not this jail mess. I look guilty already. It won't be much of a stretch for that jury to convict me prejudicially."

"I'm going to do my best to paint the picture differently to help them see something else."

Soon, the elder bailiff knocked and opened the door. His puffy grey mustache bounced with every word he spoke. "OK, Nahim, we're ready for you."

Dr. Davis was the first to stand. He grabbed Lisa's hand and helped stand her to her feet.

"OK, baby," her voice low and pensive, "here we go." She breathed a heavy sigh.

"ALL RISE! Court is now in session. The Honorable Melissa Amodie presiding." The bailiff officially heralded the start of Nahim's trial. While he stood, Nahim glanced over the audience in the courtroom. He was shocked when he noticed his father and brother in the back row. He nodded in their direction so they knew he recognized and acknowledged their presence. Tyreek gave the Black power fist and Monarch pantomimed that Nahim keep his head up. Nahim felt a surge of empowerment seeing his family in the courtroom.

Judge Amodie told everyone to sit down and began asking for "all parties in the case of the State of Louisiana vs. Nahim Lightbourne, second degree attempted murder" to stand. Lamancusa reported in "All parties for the defense present ma'am." She asked if the state was ready to begin.

"Louis Perrotta representing for the state, Your Honor."

"Please make your opening statement to the jury, Mr. Perrotta."

"Thank you, ma'am." He lifted his legal pad from the table and approached the jury box. Seven white people and five blacks comprised the jury of Nahim's peers. "Ladies and gentlemen of the jury, the State of Louisiana has charged Nahim Lightbourne with the attempted murder of Logan Potter. Mr. Lightbourne viciously attacked young Mr. Potter slamming his head into the desk with a massive blow to his head with a textbook—in full view of his classmates and teacher." Thaddeus lowered his head. "We will prove beyond the shadow of any doubt that Mr. Lightbourne brutally and maliciously tried to maim this fair teen." Perrotta leaned his head down as if grieving and then returned to his seat.

Mr. Lamancusa rose out of his seat. Before speaking, he looked at his legal pad and tapped it twice with the end of a pencil. "While Mr. Perrotta argues a cut-and-dried case, suggesting a slam dunk, but I want you ladies and gentlemen to understand the real, the story underneath the action. The cauldron that has been steeping for years that suddenly boiled over. Ma'ams and Sirs, let me ease your jobs just a bit. Nahim did in fact, hit his classmate—not with the intent to kill him nor with the intent to 'maim' him as Mr. Perrotta suggests, but I submit, he was so overwhelmed by the constant racism he endured at Hilton Preparatory Academy, he snapped, and Mr. Potter was an unfortunate casualty. So, yes, what I am saying is Mr. Lightbourne, the projected senior class valedictorian, was temporarily not in control of his faculties. I submit an affirmative conclusion, Nahim suffers from black fatigue. You will hear from psychological experts and sociologists with expertise in the study of race and racism. They will explain to you how the constant racial trauma he endured over four years since joining the student body at Hilton affected Nahim's mental capacity to control his emotional and behavioral response. What happened was a reaction that came from the many years of holding back, the years of emotional restraint from the constant name-calling, menacing and racial ridicule. Nahim, himself, is a victim. Hilton had an admirable goal of diversifying the student body, but they had not prepared the students to engage with that diversity. Nahim is the first...the first black student to walk the ivory halls of Hilton Preparatory Academy, and he bore the brunt of being black in an incredibly white space—with students who have never been confronted by another black peer—an intruder to their space." Lamancusa paced before the jury as he talked. He stopped in front of a middle-aged, sharply dressed woman and addressed her pointedly, "Black fatigue may be unfamiliar to some of you. Others of you may understand it to be the intergenerational impact of systemic racism on the physical and psychological health of Black people, which can explain why and how our society needs to collectively do more to combat its pernicious effects. In many ways, Nahim's lashing out at Logan was an act of self-defense. The widespread denial that racism rests at the root of these interconnected issues is fatiguing and literally killing those who are the victims of this system." Lamancusa turned to face Nahim's table. For years, no one could hear Nahim's silent cries. His concerns were invisible to his student peers, to the teaching staff, and to Headmaster Williams. Finally, the school hired Dr. Thaddeus Davis, who offered Nahim an empathetic ear—someone who could understand his unique needs and offer legitimate space for Nahim's development as a full human being. The only other black face in a place and space that denied his existence." He continued his statement by adding, "Hilton Prep's hiring practices or student recruitment efforts are not on trial here, but in many ways, we are making comment on the need for critical masses of disparate voices of all creeds, colors, and walks of life for the safety and emotional/mental well-being of all parties involved. To be sure, black fatigue erodes the mind, body, and spirit. I am asking you all to set aside any notions of innocent children being incapable of racist acts, but be open to the struggles of being the first." Lamancusa walked behind Nahim and patted him on the shoulder before he sat down.

Over the next several days, Perrotta and Lamancusa sparred with each other as they interviewed several academic thinkers and researchers. The judge allowed them to appear in the courtroom via Skype since they were situated in various places across the country. The experts regaled the jury and courtroom attendants with terms like microaggressions, microinsults and microinvalidations.

Sitting high in the witness stand in her Muslim hijab, Dr. Tiffenia Archie,a sociologist-turned-career-diversity- and-inclusion-specialist testified concerning "racial battle fatigue" and its effects "across the board" "disease... academically ...psychologically." She warned how "it's literally killing us." She had not talked to Nahim personally, but she said she understood what may have driven him to impassioned violence as a self-protective measure. She argued how possible it could be to "just snap."

"The people call Dr. Thaddeus Davis." Davis seemed surprised to be called. He slowly removed his arm from behind Lisa's neck where they sat in the row behind the defendant's table. The bailiff had Thaddeus swear on a Bible. "Do you promise the information you share will be the truth, the whole truth, and nothing but the truth so help you God?"

"Yes."

Perrotta begin his line of questioning. "Dr. Davis, you are a teacher at Hilton Preparatoty Academy, is that correct?"

"Yes, I teach American Studies."

"Is it safe to say your classes are fairly controversial, is that correct?"

"Controversial is a bit of a loaded term, don't you think? I prefer to think I'm providing students with the necessary cognitive dissonance that is required for learning. If that's controversial, that is not my intent."

"How long have you been on the faculty at Hilton, Dr. Davis?"

"I am concluding my first year."

"Must've been a doozy of a year. Do all your classes end up with students going to the hospital?"

"No, in all my years of teaching, this has never happened before."

"Can you describe the events in question from your vantage point?"

"Sure. We had been watching *Eyes on the Prize* for several days. It is a highly acclaimed documentary on Civil Rights Movement. We were on the fourth day of watching. Nahim had gotten upset when the video explained the killing of an unarmed black man by the state police in Alabama. His emotions were already raw with what'd been happening recently in the media. He expressed sentiments suggesting the police have a bent on killing African American men. I challenged him to keep his voice down."

"So, you persisted, even though Mr. Lightbourne was clearly hypersensitive to the video's content?"

"He wasn't the only one. Several of the other students requested we do something else because they were tired of the video."

"You continued despite their asking for an alternative method of learning?"

"Yes, I felt the video a good method for them to witness firsthand accounts of what the 1950s and 1960s was like, particularly for blacks in the American South. The entire year students had been lamenting how little their previous classes had prepared them to live and learn in an interconnected and global world. They had never really had a discussion of substance on the role and contributions of black Americans in this society. We had been making tremendous progress; the students had been making great leaps and strides in their learning. I didn't want to preclude that."

"I'm of the understanding that Headmaster Williams had forbidden you from teaching such content."

"Objection." Mr. Lamancusa wondered "Is Mr. Perrotta testifying?"

"I'm sorry, Your Honor. I'll rephrase. Dr. Davis, is it true

that Headmaster Williams had attempted to censure such addi-
tions to the curricula?"

"Yes, he had been bullied by the board to not teach the students the truth."

"So, you were teaching unapproved topics against your students' wishes and those of your boss'? Did you ever consider following the rules instead of gaslighting such impressionable young
minds?"

"Objection. Leading."

"Withdrawn. Dr. Davis, how did you get from Civil Rights
to a bleeding teenager?"

"The video turned to 'Bloody Sunday' and the march to
Selma across the Edmund Pettus Bridge. That's when Mr. Potter
chose to call Nahim 'nigger' and things went crazy. I could tell
the comment cut Nahim deeply, but I never imagined he would
lose it like he did. Of a truth, though, I can't fathom how he held
it together this long. I would have busted Logan in the head a lot
sooner."

"Objection, Your Honor."

"Sustained." Judge Amodie did not seem pleased.

"They treated that boy like garbage."

"Who did?"

"Most of those kids at Hilton. I was amazed at Nahim's
ability to hold it all together. He's a formidable young man." Davis
smiled in Nahim's direction. He caught Lisa's eye and winked at
her. She smiled and blushed back. "I'm not surprised, though. I've
heard Logan proudly use the n-word when Nahim wasn't around. I
don't think he knew I could hear him. He's right, though. He uses
that word for his friends. I don't think he and Nahim were friends
like he described, though."

"So you believe Logan is lying?"

"Umph...I won't go that far. I think he just expanded the
definition.

"Thank you, Dr. Davis. No further questions.

"Dr. Davis," Lamancusa called out while still seated,
"Would you do anything differently if you had the chance to redo
that day?"

"Truthfully, I don't know. I've rethought that day countless times. I don't think I would change my content at all. Students need to learn their history. This is not just black history, this is American history. It's all our histories."

"Thank you, Dr. Davis. No further questions." Mr. Lamancusa returned to his seat.

Chapter 30

"The people call Logan Potter." Mr. Perrotta announced the need for Logan to approach the witness stand.

Of course, he's milking it. Nahim rolled his eyes as he watched Logan's slow stroll as he gimped on his cane. It took Logan a good minute to limp to the witness stand. Nahim turned his eyes to consider how the jury judged Logan's theatrics. They certainly appeared to be moved by his labored movements—the women especially. Logan never lost their gaze. Eyes were fixed and glassy.

Mr. Perrotta approached Logan gingerly, like if he spoke too loudly, Logan would crumble to dust. Perrotta soft-balled questions to Logan asking him about his extracurricular activities and interests. He concluded by talking about Logan's loss of motor skills and physical abilities since the incident. Logan explained how he has had to change his future career plans because he is no longer able to think and process the way he had before.

Mr. Lamancusa rose to his feet as Perrotta sat down. He beelined to the witness stand and began firing questions. "Mr. Potter, is it safe to assume you don't like Nahim—have never liked Nahim?"

"What? No, 'Him is my boy!" The end of boy he elongated so it sounded like "boyeeee."

"Oh, he's your boy? WE have already heard from numerous witnesses who heard you on the day in question, refer to him as a 'nigger' and told him to 'stay in his place.' DO you often call your 'boys' the n-word?

Fumbling over his words, Logan mumbled initially, "I didn't say nigger. I said NiggA."

"What's that, Mr. Potter? I believe I heard you admit to calling Nahim a nigger."

"I said... I didn't say nigger. I said NiggA. You know like the rappers do."

"Are you a rapper, Mr. Potter?" Mr. Lamancusa straightened his tie as he addressed Logan... not quite looking at him.

"No." Logan chuckled.

"Is Mr. Lightbourne a rapper?"

"Not that I'm aware of. I've heard him rap along to music in his headphones."

"So, what gave you the idea that Nahim wanted you to address him as nigger?"

"I thought we were cool like that. I thought it'd be OK like when other blacks call each other 'brotha' instead of 'brother.'" Lamancusa lowered his voice and eyes, "So you're saying you're black, Mr. Potter?"

"Pfft. No. Can I be any whiter? I'm as white as they come." Logan blew his bangs from his eyes.

"Are you in the habit of calling all black people nigger?"

"No, just Nahim. He's the only black I know!"

"So, let me be clear. Nahim is the only black person you know—your boy—and you refer to him as a racial slur?"

"We all do. It's a word of friendship."

"Wait... wait... I assume you've had American history classes... since when was that an acceptable word of friendship?"

Mr. Lamancusa continued to grill Logan for another fifteen minutes. Logan continued to flub his words. His emotions seemed to range from exasperation to frustration to exhaustion. Mr. Lamancusa seemed to intuit Nahim's mindset that he lay off Logan out of fear of appearing like he was attacking the poor, injured boy. "one final question, Mr. Potter. What did you mean by telling Nahim to 'stay in his place?'

"I, I, I didn't mean anything. I was just playing."

"Playing, huh? No further questions, Your Honor." Lamancusa turned his back to Logan and returned to his seat.

Chapter 31

"The people call Dr. Thaddeus Aaron Davis." The bailiff's words echoed in the silent chamber.

Thaddeus sat forward removing his arm from behind Lisa's neck. His bicep flexed as his arm straightened. Lisa and Thaddeus had been holding hands. Lisa loosened her grip and patted Thaddeus' leg. "Go get 'em, babe."

"I'll do my best." He smiled his textbook grin. The bailiff asked Thaddeus about telling the truth. Of course, Thaddeus affirmed.

Mr. Perrotta approached Thaddeus in the witness stand. He stood at the front and removed his eyeglasses simultaneously pulling a handkerchief from his breast pocket. He puffed condensation on the glasses and commenced to desmudging. "Dr. Davis, you are a teacher at Hilton Preparatory Academy, is this correct?"

"Yes. Well I was. I taught high school American Studies. I was in my first year."

"I see." He puffed and wiped again this time examining the lenses. "And how long have you been doing this?"

"This was my first year at Hilton."

"My, my...a doozy of a first year, huh?"

"I should say so."

"And, it was in your classroom where the incident took place, right?" Perrotta's voice took on an air of satisfaction.

"Correct again."

"Would you mind telling the court your version of the events of that fateful day?"

"We were concluding our unit of study on the American Civil Rights Movement by watching the Eyes on the Prize video documentary. We had been watching it for about four days. I had been instructing students on the misnomer that America is a bastion of equal rights."

"I was under the impression that Headmaster Williams had

disallowed such subject matter."

"Objection. Is Mr. Perrotta testifying? The judge sustained Lamancusa's objection.

Thaddeus jumped in. "I don't mind answering that, Your Honor. Mr. Williams had been bullied by the parents and the board, in my honest opinion, into curtailing my teaching some of my instruction. Yet, I believe in academic freedom. As an educator, I have every right to teach what I believe is important. I was hired to teach American Studies, and the activities of the video occurred in Montgomery, Alabama, so I believed it was my duty, my right, and my obligation."

"So, you went against the express wishes of your boss?"

"When something is important enough. It has been said that 'Knowledge is a tree and sharing is the water element that is necessary for the growth of the tree.' When I came on board, no one had taught these kids about this history. They were starving for truth. Many of the kids reported feeling lied to in their history classes. And that is exactly what had happened. The Civil Rights journey is an episode of American history."

"So how did this history lesson turn bloody?"

"A some point during the video, Logan disrespected Nahim by calling him the n-word. Nahim didn't take it too lightly, and bashed Logan in the back of the head with his textbook, but I don't believe he intended to maim Logan or kill him. He was caught up in a moment of passion." "I can't say that I blame him either. I think Logan thought he was being friendly by using the n-word, and frankly, I don't know if I would have been able to hold it all in the way Nahim did. This was NOT new behavior. Nor was this the first time Logan had ever used that word among his peers."

"Dr. Davis, you yourself are a black man. The only black teacher at the school, correct? If it's so common, has Logan or his peers ever used this word directed at you?"

"Small peking know to keep his muff shut." Thaddeus became acutely aware he'd allowed his Liberian roots to show, although he didn't mean to. He corrected his jacket and assumed a more professional stature. "He's used it in my presence. I don't think he knew I was there, but he casually tosses that word around regularly with his boys. I've heard him say to Tyler, one of the other Hilton students, he said 'Nigger please.' I doubt he would have said it if he knew I was standing there."

The video turned towards the state police killing of Jimmie Jackson. Nahim blurted how police maltreatment of black men was commonplace. "THAT'S when Logan called him the slur and told him to stay in his place. I should have known Nahim would feel some kind of way. In that moment, I believe a wave crashed over his mind.

"And you did nothing to stop him, because you secretly harbored similar feelings because of what you 'heard' Logan say."

"Objection. He's testifying again."

"I'm sorry, Your Honor" Turning to the court reporter, "Strike my last statement."

Judge Amodie added, "Strike the counselor's last statement from the record. Objection sustained."

"Tell me, Doctor, what is your area of certification again?"

"Oh, I'm not certified at all. Hilton recruited me from my PhD program where I focused on African-American Studies."

"So, what I'm hearing is you have no professional training in education, but you felt it necessary to continue teaching a controversial, banned curriculum when even your only black student was against it and you're surprised it turned sour?"

"I didn't teach anything contrary to what they'd be getting in college. I didn't stop because the other students needed to hear 'the real.' I continued because Nahim need to know his own history. He wasn't the only one who wanted the unit over."

"So, against not only Nahim's and Mr. Williams' dissent, but several of your other students requested you forego the subject, you proceeded?"

"I sure did." Thaddeus' pride was on full display. "Those students had made such progress. They were leaps and bounds more informed than when the year began."

"Why do you think the Hilton Prep kids treated Nahim so poorly? If they did."

"That's simple. They lack the awareness of how they 'own' their spaces. Researchers have questioned how dominant groups seemed to be unaware of their 'own place of privilege in contrast to those in subordinate groups. They acknowledged that minorities had more awareness of their social status as members of an affinity group while those in dominant positions were able to recognize subordinate group status (and associated stereotypes) but identified their status simply as normal. They were also concerned with the cultural norms that directed attention away from dominant group status and privilege, a sort of bait and switch that normalizes and hides the hierarchies related to race, gender, and sexual orientation. This blindness inhibits dominants from seeing their superiority as privilege and makes dominant group status less salient. Across all tests and group identities (race, sex, sexual orientation), group membership was more salient for members of subordinated groups. Blacks and Latinos were more aware than Whites; women held more awareness than men; LGBTQ students were more aware of sexual orientation than heterosexuals. Similarly, dominant individuals held higher levels of social dominance orientation. In sum, according to the research, those with dominant group identities were largely unaware of their superior positions while group identity and status are salient matters for members of subordinate groups.

"Dr. Davis, one final question. What are your thoughts about Logan's joke that Nahim stay in his place?"

Thaddeus confidently recalled an essay he'd read. "Analysis by Simmons & Parks-Yancy (showed that students were more likely to perceive joking when the brunt of the "joke" was a member of the same race as the teacher. For instance, those who were White and had high notions of social dominance did not perceive racism when the White teacher made racial comments about White students. This was not the same for high dominance-minded whites when a Black teacher made negative racial comments towards White students, participants were offended at the notion.

"Thank you, Doctor. No further questions."
Lamancusa seized upon the energy of the moment. From his chair, he asked, "Dr. Davis, if given the option for a do-over, what would you do differently, if anything?"

"I've wracked my brain on this for weeks. I don't think I'd do anything differently. What happened to Logan is no doubt unfortunate, but what may happen to Nahim is also down-right heinous." Davis addressed the jury directly, "You let that boy go and let him have a life.

"Perrotta pleaded, "Your Honor..."

"Sustained. Witness will withdraw."

"No further questions, Judge." As Davis stood down, Judge Amodie cracked her gavel, "We'll recess until tomorrow morning at 9:00 a.m. Jury is excused."

Chapter 32

Perrotta rose and announced "The prosecution calls Jolene Young to the stand." In turn, the bailiff did his thing. Perrotta sought to understand how Jolene knew Nahim.

Jolene answered, "I met Nahim on the bus to school. He is a genuinely a nice guy. I became immediately attracted to him. I was the new girl in town and didn't really know anybody. It was good to have a friend. Imagine my surprise when I learned he is a jock. I expected him to be a conceited jerk, especially given how he's the school's basketball star. He showed me around the school and introduced me to a lot of the other kids.

When I told him my commitment to preserve my purity—that remaining a virgin was extremely important to me—he respected that and allowed me to set boundaries. We've been dating for several months now."

"Tell me about the nature of your relationship."

"He's my boyfriend, and I love him." Jolene glanced in Nahim's direction and winked at him when their eyes met. She almost said "Hi, boo," but erred on the side of caution given the circumstances. Plus, her father was seated in the gallery.
"We've heard testimony repeatedly that Nahim's race provided a barrier to his full inclusion at the school, and that many of your fellow students made it difficult for him. Is that correct?'

"I haven't really seen that. A lot of people, especially the girls," she frowned, see him as an exotic and ask to touch his hair. They say it feels like a mop. A lot of times, they don't even ask-- they just start touching. I doesn't even matter that I'm standing right there. I mean, that's just rude. I wish they would wait and get his permission first. I've seen how it makes him feel uncomfortable, but they don't care. It's like he's there toy--a plaything."

"How do you think that made him feel?"

"He's never said anything negative to me about it, but it must feel terribly alienating to be a curiosity. I know him, though, and he hates it. HE even bristles when I run my fingers through his hair. It messes up 'his waves' as he says. Do you know how many times he gets that question? He actually takes a lot of time to get his hair just right. Probably more time than me. He uses this grease stuff to condition his hair. I know when we first got together, he had to explain the rules of black hair care to me." Her face turned quizzical. "Do you know how serious they are?"

"Why do you think he's never said anything?"

"He's very concerned with coming off stereotypically. One day, I asked him why he just doesn't say 'no' when someone asks. His answer, 'Do you know how annoying and disgusting that is?' He said, 'They don't even know me. It's like I'm not even a human being who has a right to my own space.' I'm not a pet. I'm not an animal, but if I slap their hands away, I'm an angry black guy.' She explained how Nahim wasn't too offended by the first touch. "It was the hundredth that 'pressed his last nerve.' He was willing to let himself be used as a 'learning tool' for those who really wanted to understand. It's just so frustrating. In my head, I'd be screaming 'Leave my man alone!" Jolene laughed as she recalled this memory.

"Another thing that pisses me off," she winced, "Can I say that?" "was when people would tell Nahim to his face that he didn't talk black. What does that even mean? They used to say that about President Obama too. I think I remember Senator Harry Reid suggested that Obama 'had no Negro dialect--unless he wanted to have one.' Nahim was always being praised for being 'so articulate.' What, is the presumption that all black people can barely talk? Like, c'mon people, they're not all ghetto." Jolene mimicked a "black accent."

Jolene continued sharing her frustrations. "I'd especially hate it when they'd turned the stereotypes on me. Some of my girlfriends would ask privately-ish (in front of others)--'Girl, is it true what they say about black men?' I'd blush, at first, 'cause I really didn't know, but later, I was able to confirm 'I've got no complaints.'"

"You were able to confirm? What do you mean? I thought you said you were a virgin?" Jolene reacted sheepishly as she realized what she had walked herself into.

"We've played. I was curious. I'm sorry, Daddy." She looked to her father who sat slack-jawed and stupefied in the rear of the courtroom.

"So, you've had sex with Nahim?" Perrotta presumed he had Jolene cornered and pressed, "Has Nahim ever forced you to do anything you didn't want to do sexually?

Lamancusa interjected strongly, "Your Honor, I object to this whole line of questioning."

"Sustained for now. Move it along, Mr. Perrotta."

"Yes, ma'am."

"Nahim would never. He's a gentleman. I've never had to worry about him taking advantage. What we've done, I've done of my own free will. Sorry, Daddy! But you all don't know what it's like to be different at that school. Even being a 'good girl' is a bad thing. People talk."

"Thank you, Miss Young. That will be all. No further questions." Perrotta quickly returned to his seat. To Mr. Lamancusa, "Your witness, sir."

"No questions for this witness, Your Honor."

"You may step down, Miss Young. You are excused." Jolene slowly returned to sit next to her father, who appeared none too pleased.

Chapter 33

Mr. Lamancusa called Nahim to the stand. After swearing in, Nahim sat down as instructed.

"Nahim, tell us about life at Hilton Preparatory Academy." Mr. Lamancusa spoke with a calmness that set Nahim at ease, even though in the conference room Nahim added to never being so nervous.

"I never didn't have to be on. Being at Hilton meant I had to always be in the diversity spotlight. I never got a day off. Many days I went home exhausted. My mom can tell you." Nahim pointed to Lisa. "By the time I crawled into bed, I was done!" Lisa nodded in agreement--worry etched in the lines on her forehead"

"It was weird. Everyday somebody'd do something stupid to remind me of my difference, but they tried to mask it."

"What do you mean 'mask it?'"

"They'd say stuff like 'Nahim, when I look at you I don't see your color.' What the hell? To part your lips like that tells me two things. One, you're a liar. I'm 6'6". I'm a walking man mountain of brown skin. You can't help but see all this!" Nahim "showed himself" with his hands. Second, if you can say you don't see my color means you see my color. To not see it means you don't see me. You feel me? It was like that every day. They just didn't wanna see me. They were just happy when I was scoring all the points. I found myself saying, 'This is not a tanning bed accident. Momma didn't leave me in the oven too long. It doesn't wash off with bleach.' I know because I tried. Nahim seemed ashamed of himself.

"You must have been happy when Dr. Davis came to the school."

"You have no idea. Dr. D. is a G. He's become like a father to me. Sorry, Dad." Nahim genuflected towards Monarch. "It was so nice to have someone who looked like me walking the halls. And, he didn't take their bull. He commanded respect. He's the one who taught me how to be a proud black man. I didn't have to stand alone anymore. It would crack me up when the teachers would say 'Today, we're going to talk about race.' All the heads would turn towards me. I wanted to scream 'You're white! Be white!'"

"I see how that could be difficult."

"Objection. Now who's testifying?'

"Withdrawn, Your Honor."

"In all honesty, it got tougher once Dr. Davis came around."

"How so, Nahim?"

"He was putting me down on so many patterns I had been missing. These white folks were blissfully ignorant. You should have heard how they would justify all the police killings of black men. They say, 'If he would have just complied, he'd be alive.' All I heard was how Martin Luther King taught real nonviolent protest. Why can't they protest without looting and rioting?' They still shot Martin though. I got so tired of reminding them that all the mass shooting and school shootings were caused by white boys and men.

Nahim continued. "I hated being in their spotlight. The spotlight meant always being in the hot seat. When, where, how could I catch my breath? I just wanted one moment not to be someone's museum experiment. Someone's Golly. An oddity. It sucks to be the one and only. And when Logan said what he said, everything went black. I came to and they were loading him into the ambulance.

Nahim started to sob, "Oh my gosh, Logan, I didn't mean it. I'm so sorry. Can you ever forgive me?"

"Need a tissue?" Lamancusa gave Nahim a moment to compose himself.

"I'm good." Nahim sniffed.

Chapter 34

The defense rests, Your Honor." Lamancusa smoothed his tie and buttoned his sports jacket and took his seat.

"Sidebar, Your Honor?" Lamancusa wanted to speak directly to the judge.

"Counsel may approach." Lamancusa and Perrotta together walked to the judge's desk.

In a hushed tone, "Your Honor, I am not convinced the prosecution has met the standard for attempted murder. The defense requests the jury be instructed for assault."

"Mr. Perrotta?" Judge Amodie questioned the state's attorney.

"No objections, Your Honor."

"Ok, step back, gentlemen."

Judge Amodie turned to the jury. She spoke loudly, "Ladies and gentlemen, this has been a difficult case. Before we hear closing arguments and you begin deliberations, it's important that you understand your options. If you are unable to find the defendant guilty, you may consider third degree assault."

Perrotta stood and fixed his tie. "Thank you, ma'am." He inched around the outer edge of the table. "Ladies and gentlemen, we've heard already from opposing counsel, Nahim Lightbourne admits to bashing His peer, Logan Potter, in the back of the head with his textbook almost killing him. Now, according to Nahim, he 'didn't mean to hurt him', just like Logan didn't mean anything by calling Nahim a racial slur. So, who's more at fault? Can we leave it at intent?" Perrotta quick-stepped back to the table. "Nahim alleges a tense racial atmosphere that made his existence uncomfortable. But, Dr. Davis, the only other black person at the school , has not experienced this maltreatment. Are we to believe the words of an innocent boy who 'intended' to show himself friendly to someone he considered 'his boy' or the words of a THUG—who doesn't like people touching his hair--who picked up a huge book and slammed another in the back of the head so hard, he is now partially handicapped. You've heard from Dr. Bailey that had had that book hit Logan just a couple inches to the left, Logan could have been killed." For effect, Perrotta slammed a book on the table directly in front of Nahim. The thud resounded in the silent courtroom. "Two measly inches!" The echo affrighted a young woman in the gallery. She blurted a loud scream. Following his speech, Lamancusa resumed his seat. The judge dismissed the jury and adjourned the proceedings. Court officers replaced Nahim's manacles and he was led out the side door. Lisa and Thaddeus followed Mr. Lamancusa out the same door.

"So, that's it, huh?" Her voice low and melancholic.

"Now, it's a waiting game. We hope the jury comes back with a quick decision. The court will call me when the jury comes back. I'll call you. Lamancusa pulled his keys from his pocket and shook them. He sauntered down the hall to the exit—his briefcase in his left hand.

After several days of waiting, Lisa began getting very nervous. Mr. Lamancusa had explained an extended jury deliberation was a bad sign. He argued the hate crime and racism angle would be difficult to prove but he'd hope the jury would be sympathetic to their cause. The phone rang at 3:45 p.m.

"Lisa, they came back. It's so late in the day, the judge wants us in the courtroom tomorrow at 9:30."

"We'll be there. Oh, God, please protect my baby."

When they arrived at the courthouse, Lamancusa waited for them at the top of the stairs. He marched the entourage into the courtroom and directed they take their seats. Soon, Nahim was brought to the table.

"Hey, Ma."

"Hey, baby. You alright?" Lisa's voice shook but she wanted to appear strong for Nahim.

"Hey, Dr. D."

"How you holdin' up?"

"Scared. I don't know what these folks gonna do."

"I get it. I'm crossing my fingers and toes." Thaddeus' grin spoke comfort to Nahim.

Soon, both the judge and jury were seated in their respective positions. The jury foreperson had handed a folded piece of paper to Judge Amodie who quickly glanced and gave it back.

"Madam Forewoman, please read your decision."

The forewoman swallowed strongly and read. "We the people in the matter of the State of Louisiana versus Nahim Tyrone Lightbourne are hopelessly deadlocked, Your Honor." She looked disappointed. Nahim was unsure if her disappointment was related to not being able to make a decision or not being able to render a verdict altogether.

Judge Amodie questioned if the jury just needed more time. "NO ma'am. I don't think we can."

Lisa leaned forward over the railing. "What does this mean?"

"Technically, it means we've won. The jury couldn't come to a unanimous decision, so Nahim is going to get to go free. The state will be able to retry the case, but for now, we won't worry about that."

"So, he gets to go home?" Two vey heavy tears fell from her eyes.

"You hear that 'Him? You're coming home." Deep in her thoughts, Lisa sat down and exhaled. Thaddeus pulled a hankie from his inside pocket and dabbed her tears.

Postscript

Nahim's case was never re-tried. While Hilton Prep stripped his valedictory honors and disallowed him to officially walk in the graduation exercises, Nahim attended Louisiana State University majoring in English. He is writing his jail memoirs. He plans to complete his doctorate and become a tenured professor like his stepfather.

About the Author

Brian C. Johnson feels indebted to the ordinary citizens who sacrificed so much of their own personal comforts during the American Civil Rights Movement and vows to educate others while advocating for inclusive education.

Johnson is the author of "Reel Diversity: A Teacher's Sourcebook" and has edited "Glee and New Directions for Social Change." His novels include "The Room Downstairs" and "Send Judah First: the Erased Life on an Enslaved Soul."

Powder River Publishing

www.powderriverpublishing.com